MEETINGS:

Second Edition

DO'S,
DON'TS

**THE COMPLETE HANDBOOK
FOR SUCCESSFUL MEETINGS**
AND
DONUTS

Sharon M. Lippincott

**Lighthouse Point Press
Pittsburgh, Pennsylvania**

MEETINGS: DO'S, DON'TS AND DONUTS

The Complete Handbook for Successful Meetings
Second Edition

By Sharon M. Lippincott

Published by:

Lighthouse Point Press
100 First Ave., Suite 525
Pittsburgh, PA 15222

Copyright © 1999 by Sharon M. Lippincott
Printed in the United States of America
Library of Congress Catalog Card Number 98-83112

Publisher's Cataloging in Publication Data
Lippincott, Sharon M., 1944 -
Meetings: Do's, Don'ts and Donuts: The Complete Handbook for Successful Meetings, Second Edition / by Sharon M. Lippincott
       p. cm.

Includes index.
1. Meetings – Handbooks, manuals, etc.
2. Success in Business
ISBN 0-9637966-6-6: $16.95 Softcover

Book Design by John McCue Advertising Design Consultants
This book is printed on acid-free stock.

First Printing of Second Edition, February 1999

Acknowledgements
for the Second Edition

Thank you to all my colleagues, friends and helpful readers whose ideas, feedback and encouragement inspired the tweaks and additional material in this Second Edition.

Special thanks to Bernie McGinley, Ned Uber, Brien Palmer, Doug Rosensteel, Art Davidson, Janet Woodcock, Zella Soich, Ken King, and as always, to my husband, Parvin.

Table of Contents

....

Chapter One:
Introduction

....

Chapter Two:
**To Meet, or Not to Meet,
That is the Question**

....

Chapter Three:
**Planning and Preparation:
The Keys to Success**

....

Chapter Four:
Meeting Masters' Trusty Tactics   57

How to Use the Handbook

This book is not bedtime reading, and it is not a philosophical tome. It is a no-nonsense, practical, comprehensive reference manual for planning, conducting and participating in many kinds of meetings. The material is presented in self-contained units for the benefit of busy people who don't have time to read piles of theoretical books, which often stop short of useful ideas. In fact, you don't have to read the whole book at all; just read the parts you need.

To start making meetings better right now, turn to the following **Reference Guide for Troubleshooting Meetings**. Pick a problem, turn to the indicated pages with suggested solutions, and get to work.

The Handbook is divided into five sections, each beginning with a short introduction to the concepts and material covered in the section. These introductions are followed by a series of related lists of tips, guidelines, and suggestions, cross-referenced when appropriate. Each list includes a brief discussion to explain the reasoning behind the tips, and each is written to make sense and be useful by itself.

Most of the lists originated as handouts for training programs. They are helpful for individuals making personal efforts to improve meetings. They will be even more helpful when you discuss them in groups you meet with. The most dramatic results will occur when you apply the concepts covered in this Handbook throughout an organization, with top management serving as models for the rest of the company. This will initiate a change in corporate meeting culture. Heavier emphasis on individual empowerment and greater collective commitment to decisions are among the positive changes that result from widespread application.

Whatever your level of need and interest, this book will only help you make improvements if you use it. So keep it handy and refer to it often.

Troubleshooting Meetings

The Reference Guide For Troubleshooting Meetings below lists twelve of the most frequently encountered problems that occur in planning and conducting meetings. Typical causes, or sources of the problem, are listed in the middle column. The third column includes selected references to items in the Handbook addressing that particular area.

Reference Guide for Troubleshooting Meetings

Problem	Typical Causes	Handbook Reference	
Lack of focus	Unclear purpose	Reasons for Having a Meeting	22
	Poorly defined objectives	Setting Objectives	20
	Lack of agenda	Agenda Basics	43
		Sample Agenda	45
	Poorly constructed agenda		
	Poor use of agenda	How to Lead a Meeting	58
Key people don't show up	Poor scheduling	When to Meet	33
	Poor communication	Agenda Basics	43
	Lack of flexibility	Selecting Attendees	22
		Alternatives to Holding Meetings	26
		Special Agenda Considerations	47
	Unclear objectives	Setting Objectives	20

Problem	Typical Causes	Handbook Reference	
Start late/late arrivals	Agenda not predistributed	Agenda Basics Special Agenda Considerations	43 47
	Poor agenda planning		
	Negative habits	Late arrivals	84
	Lack of ground rules	Suggested Ground Rules	66
	Failure to use ground rules	How to Lead a Meeting	58
	Poor scheduling	When to Meet	33
People not prepared	Agenda not predistributed	Agenda Basics	43
	Don't know of expectations	Setting Objectives Agenda Basics	20 43
	Lack of ground rules	Suggested Ground Rules	66
	Lack of precedent Unclear delegation	Make Sure They're Ready Strategies for Effective Delegation	52 106
	Lack of follow-up	Follow-Up for Meetings	108
Meetings run overtime or out of time (cont. to next page)	Lack of agenda	Agenda Basics Special Agenda Considerations	43 47
	Poor agenda planning		
	Lack of ground rules	Suggested Ground Rules	66
	Failure to enforce ground rules	How to Lead a Meeting	58

Problem	Typical Causes	Handbook Reference	
Meetings run overtime (cont.)	Failure to get pre-meeting input	Masterful Participation	117
	Poor listening	Improve Your Listing Skills	119
	Lack of personal responsibility	Personal Preparation	114
Discussion jumps around	Lack of agenda	Agenda Basics	43
	No ground rules	Suggested Ground Rules	66
	Don't use ground rules	How to Lead a Meeting	58
	Poor listening	Improve Your Listening Skills	119
	Disorganization	Hold That Thought	88
Indiv- iduals dominate	Lack of ground rules	Suggested Ground Rules	66
	Lack of leadership	Role of the Meeting Leader	58
	Weak facilitation	Role of the Meeting Leader / Keep the Discussion On Track	58 / 86
	Poor listening	Improve Your Listening Skills	119
	Gender-related communication style differences	Genderspeak	132
Arguments during meetings (cont. to next page)	Unclear objectives	Clarifying Objectives	20
	Lack of personal preparation	Make Sure They're Ready / Personal Preparation	52 / 114
	Lack of ground rules	Suggested Ground Rules	66

Problem	Typical Causes	Handbook Reference	
Arguments during meeting (cont.)	Weak facilitation	How to Lead a Meeting	58
	Poor listening	Improve Your Listening Skills	119
	Personality differences	The Clock is Running Resolving Conflict	91 101
Griping and negativity	Lack of ground rules	Suggested Ground Rules	66
	Failure to establish a positive climate	How to Lead a Meeting Meeting Climate Climate Control	58 63 103
	Poor listening	Improve Your Listening Skills	119
	Wrong people included	Selecting Attendees	22
Decisions always delayed	Agenda not predistributed	Agenda Basics	43
	No pre-meeting conferences	Masterful Participation	117
	Lack of personal preparation	Make Sure They're Ready Personal Preparation	52 114
	Poor listening	Improve Your Listening Skills	119
	Lack of empowerment	Strategies for Effective 　　Delegation Dealing with Indecisiveness	106 136
Nothing happens as a result (cont. to next page)	Lack of agenda	Agenda Basics	43
	Weak delegation	Strategies for Effective 　　Delegation	106
	Lack of commitment	How To Generate Consensus	142
	Lack of follow-through	Follow-Up for Your Meetings	108

Problem	Typical Causes	Handbook Reference	
Nothing happens (cont.)	Incomplete problem-solving	Tips for Unblocking Stuck Meetings Dealing With Indecisiveness Plan-Do-Check-Act Brainstorming Guidelines Brainstorming Variations	100 136 144 146 150
	Lack of organizational support	Strategies for Effective Delegation Dealing with Indecisiveness	106 136
Meetings taking up too much time for individuals	Failure to clarify objectives	Setting Objectives Which Meetings to Attend	20 28
	Lack of creative scheduling	Selecting Attendees Alternatives to Holding Meetings Special Agenda Considerations	22 26 47
	Over-commitment	Opting Out	29

Summary of Principles

....

Principle #1:
> *Be discerning about the need for meetings.*

....

Principle #2:
> *Plan meetings with purpose.*

....

Principle #3:
> *Use meeting ground rules to maintain focus, respect, and order.*

....

Principle #4:
> *Take personal responsibility for meeting outcomes.*

....

Principle #5:
> *If your meeting isn't working, try another tool.*

1

Introduction

"Have I been stood up, or did I write the date down wrong?" I asked myself this question as I sat in a donut shop, waiting for a colleague. We had scheduled this afternoon meeting to discuss a project for a professional organization. When he finally arrived, fifteen minutes late, he was flustered, and full of apologies. He had just left the bi-weekly meeting of his company's Quality Council.

"I seem to spend my whole life in meetings these days," he groaned. "The Quality Council meets twice a month. I sit on several task forces and committees connected with quality, not to mention all the meetings it takes just to get my regular work done. Then, half my evenings are spent in meetings of community or professional organizations. The issues are important, but most of the time nothing gets resolved, so most of these meetings are a big waste of time. I'm ready to move to Fiji!"

Do you feel the same way? You aren't alone! People all over the country are missing deadlines and dropping the ball on urgent work because of all the time they spend in meetings. Many of these meetings are poorly conducted, with attendees walking into them cold and uninformed about the issues. Some are held more from habit than need. Others are held, and attended, largely for political reasons. These meetings are especially likely to crackle with confrontation as people vie to promote personal agendas. Too many poorly run meetings spawn more just like them, because nobody is prepared to make a decision or take action.

In spite of the frustration meetings can cause, nobody would seriously suggest their wholesale abandonment. For better or worse, meetings make the world go around – at least the business world. Most people agree that meetings are necessary to coordinate individual efforts, collaborate on joint projects, garner support for causes, sell ideas, collectively solve problems or make decisions, and make judgments about people with whom you work.

Meetings are profoundly important to you personally. They're the stage you perform on. Nobody sees you alone in your office crunching numbers or hammering out reports. Others may benefit from good work you do on these private projects, but you benefit from relationships built in meetings. People see you in action during meetings, and form opinions about your competence based on the way you conduct yourself and your business there.

Nearly any meeting can be improved and made more successful. Many talented people have discovered ways to make meetings more beneficial for all concerned. Their successful efforts make these "Meeting Masters" stand out in the grateful memory of their colleagues.

Meeting Masters realize that they bear personal responsibility for the success of every meeting they attend, even when someone else schedules or conducts the meeting. They know how to cut through chaos to find the issues that really matter. They plan and conduct meetings to address these issues, then facilitate decisions, and follow through to get results. Meetings they attend focus more sharply on objectives, proceed more smoothly and take less time than usual, even when they don't sit in the leader's seat.

That doesn't mean these meetings are always short. Some meetings need to be conducted free of heavy time-pressure. When you are forming consensus, settling differences, or solving problems, haste is counter-productive. Even in ordinary meetings that stay focused, allowing time for an occasional joke or story relieves tense moments and increases rapport.

Meeting Masters achieve their great results through a combination of specific skills and behaviors, together with the wisdom for knowing when to use them. The good news is that anyone can learn to think like a Meeting Master and use these skills. This Handbook has been written to help people do just that. It is full of tips collected over many years of observing

Meeting Masters in action, interviewing them, and collecting accounts of their results. These observations have been coupled with the latest published meeting management strategies. The result is a collection of tips on how to improve the outcomes of meetings, how to avoid meetings that are not worth attending, and how to tell the difference between the two.

Suggested strategies cover every aspect of the meeting process, beginning with help in deciding whether to have or attend a meeting. They include tips for planning and preparing the agenda, conducting and participating in meetings, and follow-up strategies which ensure lasting results. Guidelines are given to help both leaders and other participants. There are even tips on Back Seat Leadership for occasions when the leader isn't firmly in the saddle.

Whatever your current level of expertise, these guidelines can help you improve meetings you attend. Those who have already achieved the status of Meeting Master know that all meetings benefit from a continuous improvement process. They will find new ideas here for ways to liven up and fine tune meetings. People who currently dread meetings, or take them for granted, will find a wealth of information on ways to make positive changes at any level, from making a more effective personal contribution to completely restructuring the meeting culture of a whole organization.

2

To Meet, or Not to Meet, That is the Question

Sally chairs a scholarship committee for a service organization. This committee has existed for longer than anyone can remember, with regular monthly meetings faithfully held. She recently realized that there is very little business to attend to, except during the two or three months of the year when applications are screened. Most of the meetings are poorly attended, and basically a waste of time. She is thinking about canceling all meetings that serve no direct purpose for administration or promotion of scholarships.

Chris, the marketing director for a large law firm, has already attended five meetings in the first three days of this week, and just got a call about another. The latest one, to be held first thing tomorrow morning, is being called to solve a problem that suddenly surfaced in another department. Chris really doesn't have time to attend, and suspects his input is irrelevant. He is strongly tempted to beg off.

Sally and Chris are on the right track as they think about their respective meetings, but neither of them is quite sure how to justify following their instincts. They'll be happy to learn they can do what seems right, without feeling guilty. Many meetings don't need to be held in the first place, and most of the rest are attended by more people than necessary.

Principle #1:
Be discerning about the need for meetings.

19

There are two levels of decisions to be made about scheduling and attending a meeting. First, the person in charge must decide whether it is worth having, or if the need can be better met some other way. Then, if a meeting is scheduled, people who are requested to attend must decide whether to attend all or part of the meeting, or perhaps skip the whole thing. This section includes guidelines for making sound decisions about the importance of meetings.

Setting Objectives

Since meetings are only a means to an end, keep that end result firmly in mind as you define objectives for the group or yourself. These simple questions will help clarify your meeting objectives, whether you are planning the overall meeting, or preparing to participate in one:

- Why am I scheduling (or choosing to participate in) the meeting?

- What do I want to accomplish as a result of the meeting?

- What information will be exchanged, plans formulated, or decisions made in this meeting?

- Who will be there that I need to influence or whose support I need to gain?

Examples of Clear Objectives

- To brainstorm ways of improving the quality of customer service.

- To generate consensus on new housekeeping standards.

- To make recommendations to the C.F.O. about alternative accounting services.

- To convince the board to adopt a new project.

How to Tell if a Meeting is Really Necessary

After defining your objectives, consider carefully whether holding a meeting is really the best way to handle the situation. Make sure it will be a good use of time for all concerned. In general, a meeting will have value if it performs at least one of these functions:

- **Communication**
  When several people need to hear or discuss the same information, a meeting is a good option. It can save time and avert misunderstanding.

- **Exercising Persuasion**
  Sometimes it is easier and faster to generate widespread support for an idea in a group. Other times, you need the support of others to convince an individual of the merit of a proposal.

- **Solving Problems**
  The diversity of perspectives provided by a group can be an invaluable resource for problem-solving. Some examples of problem-solving functions that benefit from differences of opinion and perspective include accurate definition of problems, brainstorming, and identifying innovative resources.

- **Making Decisions**
  When the whole group bears responsibility for supporting a decision, consensus is the recommended strategy. Consensus is especially effective for making decisions that require strong personal commitment to implement or enforce (see page 142).

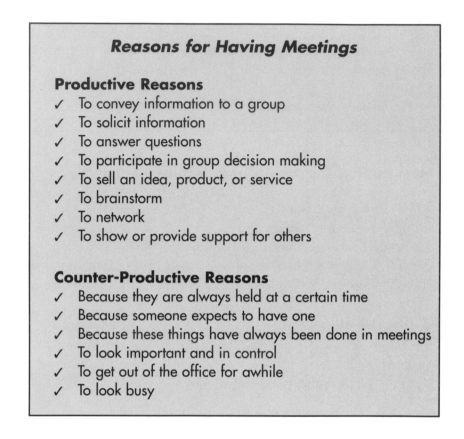

Reasons for Having Meetings

Productive Reasons
- ✓ To convey information to a group
- ✓ To solicit information
- ✓ To answer questions
- ✓ To participate in group decision making
- ✓ To sell an idea, product, or service
- ✓ To brainstorm
- ✓ To network
- ✓ To show or provide support for others

Counter-Productive Reasons
- ✓ Because they are always held at a certain time
- ✓ Because someone expects to have one
- ✓ Because these things have always been done in meetings
- ✓ To look important and in control
- ✓ To get out of the office for awhile
- ✓ To look busy

Selecting Attendees

Selecting the right people to attend a meeting is crucial to its success. As the number of participants grows, the cost of the meeting rises rapidly. Including more people also means the discussion is likely to be prolonged, and each person will have less opportunity to participate. Yet, excluding certain types of people, for example, those with critical information, is likely to slow things down or create problems later.

A good rule of thumb is to include only people who can be directly helpful in making decisions and achieving the objective of the meeting. When you will be making major decisions, it is also wise to include someone to represent those who will be affected by them.

A challenge arises when the number of helpful and/or affected people exceeds eight or ten. If the number climbs above this point, consider subdividing your objectives and holding separate meetings with more narrowly focused groups. Larger groups can be productive if you have expert facilitation (see page 137). You can also use techniques such as break-out groups with larger groups to give maximum opportunity for participation.

Use the guidelines below to first limit your list to the most productive participants, and then to make sure you didn't overlook any important additions:

- **Assistance**
  Who can help you achieve your objective?

- **Power**
  Who has the power to make decisions, and the responsibility for implementing them?

- **Support**
  Who supports your objective?

- **Undecided**
  Who may be on the fence?

- **Opposition**
  Who opposes your objective?

- **Interference**
  Who may cause trouble if not included?

- **Obligation**
  Who are you obliged to invite?

Calculating the Cost

People are often staggered to learn the true cost of meetings. For example, a two-hour meeting involving six professionals, with an average hourly value of $55 per person, costs the company $660, just for the time involved. When preparation and follow-up time, supplies, overhead for the meeting room, etc., are added, the cost easily zooms above $1,000. In a company with a management team of 50 people, who each attend an average of 20 such meetings per month, the monthly cost of these meetings is over $150,000. It is ironic that elaborately documented purchase orders and several layers of approval are usually required to purchase an office item costing less than $100, but no thought is given to justifying the cost of meetings.

The return on the investment of time/money in a meeting will depend on the value of the results produced, together with the efficiency of the meeting process. Obviously, meetings that are well-planned and smoothly run are likely to produce better results in a shorter time and be more cost-effective. But, however well run, not all meetings are a good investment. Understanding the full price of a meeting will help you objectively weigh costs and benefits, and know when to bypass the meeting in favor of an alternative strategy. Awareness of meeting cost also provides powerful motivation for keeping meetings concise.

The form on the next page provides an outline for calculating the cost of a meeting. To use the form, list the people you expect to include in the left-hand column. Enter the value of each participant's time in the second column. For a business meeting, that may be the billable rate, or the full cost to the company of keeping that person employed. This is roughly double the person's salary – counting benefits, overhead for office space and equipment, etc. Estimate time value if you aren't sure. Multiply the time value for each person by the expected length of the meeting (entered in column three), and put this figure in the right hand column. Then add all entries in the right-hand column to determine the total cost for all participants. Add estimated additional time for preparation, supplies, space, etc., to determine the total overall cost of the meeting.

Meeting Cost Calculator

Attendees	Time Value	X Length	Total Cost
1.			
2.			
3.			
4.			
5.			
6.			
7.			
8.			
9.			
10.			
Total Cost for Attendance			
Other Costs			
Prep Time (all involved)			
Speaker or Other Resource People			
Prep Costs (mailing, etc.)			
Handouts			
Visuals, etc.			
Room Costs			
Refreshments (if served)			
Transportation Costs for Attendees			
Other			
Total Meeting Cost			

Alternatives to Holding Meetings

There is often a better way to meet your objectives than having a meeting. Below is a list of creative alternatives to unnecessary meetings:

- **Phone Calls**
  When you need advice, opinions, or information from a small number of people, phone calls can do the job. They avoid tying up group time for conversations that only involve one or two other people. Conference calls with two or three other people can eliminate travel time when people are in scattered locations. They are a good choice for simple discussions.

- **Memos or Letters**
  Correspondence is the simplest way to provide information to large numbers of people. Sometimes correspondence is needed even when you do have a meeting. When detailed information will be covered in a meeting, some form of premeeting briefing material should be distributed to allow time to study the issues before discussing them. This makes meetings far more efficient and productive, and often avoids the need for follow-up sessions.

- **Water Cooler Conversations**
  Bumping into people in the lunchroom, hallway, or health club can yield a wealth of information that might be difficult to obtain in a meeting. Most people find it easier to speak candidly in a casual encounter. During meetings, political considerations often stifle free expression, resulting in a phenomenon called Group Think. Group Think is characterized by a tendency to stick to politically correct opinions, and it generally inhibits effective decisions. Knowing people's inclinations ahead of time helps prevent Group Think, so many Meeting Masters make it a point to be in the right place at the right time to have seemingly spontaneous conversations. These chats take the place of some formal meetings and help prepare for others.

- **Remote Location Brainstorming**
  By using written input and other innovative techniques, lots of good ideas can be collected and processed by a group without ever convening a meeting (see page 150).

- **Delegate**
  There are several reasons why delegation may be the best way to meet a need (see page 107). For example, you may not be the best person to handle this issue. Even if you are, you may not have time. Delegation is also an appropriate way to empower and train subordinates.

- **Do it Yourself**
  Don't waste time calling a meeting to seek input when you really don't plan to use it. Calling meetings to evade personal responsibility, or to fake the appearance of listening, sabotages morale.

When Change is Unwelcome

Not many people will be upset to hear that a meeting is canceled. Yet, now and then, you will encounter serious resistance when you decide to tamper with history and abandon a meeting schedule or format that no longer meets current needs.

Listen to the objections carefully (see page 119). Clarify them as much as possible, because there may be a valid reason among them. Most will reflect needs that may be met some other way, such as the following:

- **Social Events**
  Although the original mission may have long since been achieved or forgotten, members still enjoy the opportunity to visit.

- **Comfort of Routine**
  People take comfort in routine and tradition, and often resist change.

- **Bonus Dividends**
  People depend on the structure of the meeting to facilitate associations that have unrelated benefits.

- **Hidden Agendas**
  Somebody is getting political mileage out of the meetings for purposes other than those stated.

Rut Buster techniques are useful for coping with the first two situations (see page 134). In the latter two, you may need to be creative to identify the unstated personal objectives and find a way of either aligning them with the overall objectives or meeting them some other way. In any instance, work with the people involved to find alternatives that present a positive outcome for all concerned.

Which Meetings to Attend

Ideally, you should not attend a meeting unless you can make a valid contribution to a successful outcome, or further your own purposes. Since a successful outcome may also include factors of political expediency, the best choice about attending isn't always obvious. The following questions will help you decide when to attend and which meetings to ditch.

- **Obligation**
  Are you formally obligated to attend, i.e., membership on a board?

- **Providing Information**
  Do you have valuable information to present about an item on the agenda?

- **Obtaining Information**
  Do you need to obtain information from the group?

- **Researching Issues**
  Can you benefit from learning other people's thoughts on an issue?

- **Outcomes**
  Will the outcome of the meeting directly affect you or a project in which you are involved?

- **Solving Problems**
  Can your expertise help solve a worthwhile problem?

- **Relationships**
  Can you build or nurture an important relationship?

- **Politics**
  Is attendance politically correct?

If you answer yes to two or more questions, the meeting should be worth attending. If you answered yes only once, consider alternatives. If none of the answers were positive, politely make your excuses.

Opting Out

Double check for surprise items on the agenda before you decide not to attend a meeting. Then, if you do decide to skip it, use one of these alternatives to handle the situation:

- **Tell the Truth**
  Honesty is the best policy when explaining your decision not to attend, but you can choose what to be honest about.

- **Written Input**
  If all you are doing is providing simple input, a memo or written report may suffice.

- **Suggest an Alternative**
  There may be an alternative way to fulfill the overall objectives without actually having a meeting, i.e., e-mail, teleconferencing, or delegation of responsibility (see page 26).

3

Planning and Preparation: The Keys to Success

Upon returning from a meeting, Lonnie found a message that Lou had called to schedule a meeting with their project team. Lonnie left a message on Lou's voice mail, agreeing to show up at the specified time, a week later.

When the meeting began, nobody knew where to start. Crucial time was wasted as people returned to their offices for material they hadn't anticipated needing, or made calls to get more information. Further interruptions occurred when two members were summoned to their offices to take care of "emergencies." The meeting was finally adjourned, with a follow-up session scheduled for three days later. Nothing had been accomplished. Six people had wasted nearly two hours each, and everyone felt frazzled.

What happened? Basically, nothing. In fact, that's the problem. Good meetings don't just happen any more than a ship just happens to float itself across the ocean from one continent to another. Whether the meeting involves two people or two hundred, if it's going to be a success, somebody has to take charge, planning and organizing the event ahead of time.

Principle #2:
Plan meetings with purpose.

Many functions are involved in planning and preparing for a successful meeting. These include identifying a time and place, drafting and distributing an agenda, and making sure participants have everything they need to personally prepare. Participants should review the agenda and any background material to prepare for productive participation. Depending on your role in the meeting, you may also need to ensure support for important issues.

Meeting Masters heavily emphasize preparation. For example, one, who believes no meeting should last more than an hour, chairs a committee that handles requests for assistance from a charitable organization. He prepares an agenda and packets of information about the current requests and sends this material to all committee members at least a week before the meeting. The members are expected to study each request ahead of time and find answers to any questions. This procedure has cut the length of their meetings from over three hours to less than one. Furthermore, in spite of the fact that the committee is handling more requests than ever, individual members seldom spend more than half an hour preparing, so everyone is saving time.

More commonly, meeting leaders are like Jack, the busy president of a community organization. They believe that other commitments make it impossible to spend time preparing for meetings. When someone suggested to Jack that board meetings would go more smoothly with some advance preparation, he claimed, "There's no way I can spend that much time on this organization!" So board meetings continued to ramble and run overtime, and half the members didn't bother to show up for any given meeting. Jack's pet project was voted down, and the whole organization drifted into a state of apathy. When his term was up, Jack dropped out of the organization.

On the surface, it may appear that planning is a further burden for these individuals. Planning does take a certain amount of time, but there are alternatives. The burden of planning doesn't have to fall fully on the leader's shoulders. The leader is responsible for seeing that the planning gets done, not necessarily for doing it. Every step can be delegated (see page 106). Just be sure that when you have delegated the planning for a meeting you will conduct, you are thoroughly familiar with the agenda, objectives, and any relevant background information before the meeting begins.

Sometimes participants find it convenient to act as ad hoc meeting planners. If you realize that nothing is being done to organize a meeting you will be attending, be a Back Seat Leader. Request the information you need, and/or offer to help prepare it. The time you spend up front may pay off in major savings later by avoiding the need for follow-up meetings.

Sarah filled this ad hoc role for an organization similar to Jack's. When it became clear that the president was not a strong organizer, she offered to plan the agenda and contact members. The delighted president then had nothing to do but preside over a smoothly run meeting. Sarah's efforts paid off. She was elected president the next year, and she later became state president of the organization. Her career has prospered nicely as a result of that honor, which reflected her skill as a Meeting Master.

The guidelines in this section will steer you through the preparation process for any meeting, whether you are the designated leader, Back Seat Leader, or simply a savvy participant.

When to Meet

The choice of meeting time depends on factors such as your purpose for meeting, the availability of key people and availability of appropriate facilities. The anticipated length of the meeting will also be a factor. For example, if you know everyone is used to eating lunch around 12:00, it wouldn't make sense to start a two-hour staff meeting at 11:30 a.m.

Helpful Hint

Schedule your meetings for odd times like 10:06. These unusual times will catch people's attention, making them easier to remember, and more likely to be taken seriously.

Sometimes the timing is a given. For example, short sales meetings are often held first thing in the morning to distribute new assignments and generally get everyone prepared for the day. Production staff meetings are likely to be held either before or after shift hours to avoid interfering with line duties. Employees who have lots of contact with customers generally don't schedule meetings during the time customers are most available or likely to call.

When the decision on timing is flexible, the considerations listed in the following table will help you make a choice:

Time	Advantages	Disadvantages
First Thing in the Morning	People will be fresh and less likely to be preoccupied with other business.	With the whole day ahead, the meeting may run overtime.
Late Morning	People in the meeting may be more focused by the motivation to finish before lunch.	If attendance isn't mandatory, people may skip the meeting to meet noon deadlines, or they may be distracted by urgent tasks or earlier events.
Early Afternoon	Some people will have hit their stride for the day and be quite productive.	Some people feel lethargic after lunch.
Late Afternoon	People can feel finished for the day with their earlier work, and will be eager to keep the meeting from running past quitting time.	People may feel pressured by the events of the day, or just plain tired. Their fear of running late and not being able to leave on time may cause them to agree to decisions they don't fully support, or to with-hold important information. These actions may shorten the meeting, but cause long-lasting negative effects.

Time	Advantages	Disadvantages
Evening (for non-job-related meetings)	Doesn't usually interfere with job.	May interfere with family and personal activities. People may be too tired to be objective, cooperative, etc.
Outside Working Hours (for job-related meetings)	Doesn't interfere with routine, time-sensitive tasks, such as answering phone calls or working on a production line.	If no additional compensation is given, or no substantial benefits result, frequent mandatory meetings outside working hours create resentment.

Helpful Hint

If you plan to begin a meeting first thing in the morning, allow a few minutes after the designated start of the day for people to get settled, pour coffee, and recuperate from the pressures of commuting. Although first thing Monday morning is often chosen as an ideal staff meeting time, it may not give best results. Absenteeism is often higher on Monday mornings, and the pressures of commuting more stressful on Mondays than other mornings through the week. Consider the advantages of holding your meeting later in the day, or on a different day altogether.

Where to Meet

The choice of a meeting place has a major effect on the success of the meeting. Sometimes the choice is obvious, for example committee meetings that must be held in a conference room because everyone works in cubicles, or staff meetings that are always held in the manager's office. Other meetings require special consideration. The following guidelines will help you decide where to meet:

- **Minimize Distractions**
  Regardless of the size and purpose of your meeting, interruptions and phone calls will slow it down and may derail it entirely. Choose a place where you can close the door and hold all calls. When meeting in a restaurant, arrange for seating out of the main traffic flow.

- **Territorial Considerations**
  This is a little like "home court advantage." When equality is an issue, meet on neutral ground, such as a conference room, restaurant, or off-site facility. Your office lends a personal touch, but if you are asking a favor, or trying to exercise persuasion, going to the other person's office may tip the scale in your favor.

- **Comfort Factor**
  Beware of overly comfortable chairs when you want to keep things moving. Conversely, when the meeting is inherently long and arduous, select seating that provides an acceptable degree of comfort.

- **Equipment**
  Be sure any special equipment, such as a rear-projection system, can be used at the chosen location.

- **Convenience**
  Try to balance the time and distance required for participants to get to the meeting. Consider parking, accessibility to major roads and similar factors when travel is involved.

- **Commercial Facilities**
  For a very important presentation, training session, or lengthy meeting, a hotel or other professional meeting facility will provide comfort, image, and other positive factors.

- **Room Arrangements**
  A conference table is desirable for group discussions.
  Whatever seating arrangement you select, be sure to allow
  for eye contact between as many people as possible. If you
  have subcommittees or break-out groups as part of your
  meeting design, be sure there is ample room for them to
  hold discussions without distracting each other. Individual
  break-out rooms are ideal.

Meeting Over Meals

Mealtime meetings tend to have more social overtones and less
emphasis on business. This can be a distinct advantage if your
objective is to build rapport and nurture relationships, but
beware of distractions and unexpected occurrences that make
it difficult to keep a discussion focused. Keep paperwork to
a minimum to avoid table clutter and soiled papers. If there is
a lot of paperwork involved, meet for business at your office,
and adjourn to the restaurant, or vice-versa.

A summary follows of factors to consider in making decisions
about meal-based meetings:

- **Breakfast**
  Tends to be more direct and focused, less likely to ramble.
  People may be more easily available. This is a good informal
  brainstorming time for anyone but night owls, who may not
  be fully alert until after 10 a.m. and several cups of coffee.

- **Lunch**
  Good for quick networking and building relationships.
  Restaurants may be busy and loud; service may be slow.
  People may be concerned about getting back to work on
  time. Between social amenities and the mechanics of ordering,
  business may be slow to start and end up rushed and
  incomplete. If your schedules are flexible, late lunches can
  avoid much of the rush.

- **Dinner**

  Little real business gets conducted over dinner. People are tired and less clear-headed at the end of the day. An expensive meal encourages socializing and promotes lingering, which makes it a great way to pamper a Very Important Customer, especially one from out-of-town.

- **Membership Meetings**

  This type of meeting lends itself well to meal meetings any time of the day. For many people, networking is a major objective of these meetings, and the time spent eating offers a good opportunity to pursue this activity. Keep any business meeting minimal at these functions.

Types of Meetings

Meetings can be grouped into six general types, each of which serves a specific purpose and has slightly different implications for planning. Many meetings combine two or more types, requiring a blending of techniques. The types are listed in the following table, together with a description of their purpose:

Type	Purpose	Planning Considerations
Task-Oriented	Held by task forces and various types of work teams to review progress on projects, and define new assignments in cooperation with other team members.	Arrange to have necessary information and resources at meeting. Provide appropriate background information ahead of time.
Problem-Solving	Held to analyze alternatives and generate solutions. Meeting to negotiate an agreement is a form of problem-solving.	Define problem as well as possible ahead of time to allow people time to think and gather information about proposed solutions. Have flip chart and other tools. May benefit from off-site location.

Type	Purpose	Planning Considerations
Creativity/ Innovation	Held to brainstorm improvements and innovations (see page 146). Creativity/ innovation techniques are often used in problem-solving meetings.	Similar to problem-solving meetings. Extended sessions pose additional considerations (see page 50).
Communication	Held to present information such as reports, announcements, or new product information, or to request information, network, etc. They may involve two-way communication or be used strictly to receive or convey information.	Special attention to presentation format and supporting visual and handout material. For information gathering, brief participants ahead of time on expectations, and prepare a checklist of questions and items to be covered.
General Purpose	Held to address a variety of objectives, incorporating elements of several different meeting types. Includes most staff meetings, board meetings, etc. (see page 155).	Prepare appropriately for each objective, using suggestions for matching meeting type.
Policy Definition	Held to cooperate on implementing or redefining policies that affect many people or different departments. They may incorporate elements of communication, problem-solving, and creativity/ innovation meetings.	Meticulous pre-meeting communication and briefing. See suggestions above for problem-solving preparation, etc.

Leadership Issues

The type of leadership to be used for your meeting is another planning factor. Meetings are ordinarily led by officially designated people, such as managers, chairpersons, or team leaders, but other choices may be appropriate. For example, the obvious person may be unavailable or unsuitable for one reason or another, and an alternate may be appointed.

The choice of leadership also depends on the type of meeting. Meetings that involve planning, brainstorming, consensus formation, or problem-solving often intensify natural inclinations to promote personal interests, or conversely, to fall prey to Group Think and say what they think the leadership wants to hear. In cases like this, it is especially important to have a skilled facilitator in charge of the discussion (see page 137).

When you use a facilitator, the designated meeting leader opens the meeting, takes care of any unrelated or preliminary business, then introduces the facilitator. Once the facilitator takes charge, the leader participates on a par with the other group members.

The facilitator, or other designated leader, will need to prepare for the meeting, just as the rest of the participants do. These guidelines will help you work productively with any alternate leader:

- **Review the Agenda**
  Someone who is thoroughly familiar with the agenda should meet with the facilitator to explain each item in depth, including background information. Be sure to mention any undercurrents or divisions of opinion that are likely to be a factor in the discussion.

- **Clarify Process**
  Discuss the preferred way for handling each item with the facilitator. In many instances, the facilitator may have suggestions for better ways to deal with a particular problem. The selected approach should be explained to the group before it is used.

● **Define Equipment Needs**
The facilitator may suggest items such as flip charts, overhead projectors, or other equipment that will be helpful during the meeting. Facilitators generally assume the responsibility of arranging for the equipment and making sure it is in the meeting room, but that responsibility is negotiable. Just make sure someone is in charge.

● **Appoint a Monitor**
It may be helpful to appoint a monitor or assistant to the facilitator (see Helpful Hint, page 61). In a large and lively group, the facilitator can get so busy managing ideas and information that it is hard to pay adequate attention to factors like individual participation. To make sure nobody is ignored, or lacks the chance to contribute, designate a group member to watch specifically for lack of participation, nonverbal signs of reservations, etc. (see page 94).

Other Roles

Many roles besides that of leader contribute to the success of a meeting. The number and nature of roles to be filled depends on the purpose and complexity of the meeting. Ideally, these roles should be defined during the planning stage, and people selected to fill them should be alerted ahead of time.

Use the list below to help decide which roles will be helpful for your meeting, adding others as the need is identified:

● **Recorder**
Whether or not your meeting requires that official minutes be kept, it is helpful to have a designated person take notes (see page 78). These can be referred to during the meeting to keep track of complex discussions or agenda decisions. When copied and distributed, they provide a uniform record for participants.

- **Presenter**
  When specific information is required or reports will be delivered, check with the presenters in advance. Make sure they are aware of objectives or expectations for their presentations and agree that they are appropriate.

- **Time-keeper**
  Not every meeting requires a time-keeper, but when participants tend to be verbose, such a person can be helpful, even in small groups. You can appoint a time-keeper at the outset of the meeting, but alerting someone in advance will ensure that they have an appropriate watch or clock (see page 91).

- **Discussion Leader**
  Advance notice allows the discussion leader to review the material in advance and make appropriate preparations. This is important whether you have a member of the group leading a portion of the discussion, or use a formal facilitator for the whole meeting (see page 137).

- **Monitor**
  Many meeting leaders find it helpful to appoint someone with keen observation skills to keep an eye on the participation process during a meeting. This frees the leader to focus on the task-oriented meeting content (see Helpful Hint box on page 61).

- **Evaluator**
  Groups that are intent on improving their process and performance will benefit from appointing a formal meeting evaluator. This evaluator gives personal insights and conducts a brief group evaluation (see page 110).

● **Miscellaneous**
   In a well-planned meeting, every person serves a purpose.
   Make sure each person knows what that purpose is.

Agenda Basics

The meeting agenda serves three purposes:

1) The thought involved in drafting an agenda clarifies the
   objectives, and may identify pre-meeting strategies that
   increase effectiveness.

2) Circulating the agenda ahead of time helps participants plan
   and prepare to make an effective contribution.

3) During the meeting, the agenda provides direction and
   focus for the discussion and serves as a reference point for
   the discussion leader or facilitator.

   Meetings without an agenda are like a ship on the ocean
with no map or compass. Just as there are different sorts of
maps and navigational instruments for different situations, there
are different formulas for creating effective agendas. The form and
content may be tailored to suit the purpose and type of meeting,
but regardless of the form, there are some basic elements
that need to be addressed. To formulate an agenda with power
and impact, make sure it includes the components listed below:

● **Title**
   Give the meeting a name to emphasize the reason for
   having it.

- **Time, Date, and Location**
  Let people know when and where to show up. Highlight any changes from standard routine. To make sure changes are noticed, highlight them with a colored marker.

- **Mission and Objectives**
  Tell people why the meeting is being held, including both the general purpose and specific objectives.

- **List of Participants**
  Help attendees prepare by letting them know who is expected to attend and, if anyone doesn't already know, the reason each is included.

- **Roles of Participants**
  Notify participants of what each is expected to contribute to the meeting process.

- **Discussion Items**
  Include the following information for each agenda item:

  - Description

  - Goal or desired outcome (if appropriate)

  - Relevant background information, i.e., minutes of past meetings, briefing material, etc.

  - Time allocation for discussion

  - Name of person responsible for covering each item during the meeting.

Helpful Hint

Be careful not to overload any given meeting with too many objectives (see page 20). Consider how long people will be able to mentally stay on track, and whether any specific items will overshadow other important ones. It may be better to have more than one meeting than to try to accomplish too much at one time.

Sample Agenda

The following sample agenda has been drafted for a meeting with a management group. The group has already discussed this project at several previous meetings. At this meeting, the project task team, which was appointed by the group, is scheduled to present their final report and recommendations. Following the presentation, the report will be discussed by the managers in attendance.

Lee Smith, the meeting leader, has already contacted attendees by phone to determine their availability for this meeting and to clarify their respective roles and contributions. This agenda is being sent, together with a copy of the team report, to remind everyone of the meeting and the format. Since the group's ground rules mandate that members be familiar with background material before the meeting, they will be prepared for an active discussion. The consensus process is likely to proceed smoothly, with few surprises.

DATE: March 27, 1999
TO: Staff and Project Team Members
FROM: Lee Smith
RE: DESIGN REVIEW MEETING
July 10, 1998, 9 a.m.
Conference Room D

Meeting Mission: To review proposed design changes in the X-009 model.

Objective: To generate consensus about beginning production of updated model by September 1.

Attendees: Pat Johnson, Management; George Parr, Engineering; John Andrews, Manufacturing; Susan Jenner, Marketing; Ron Mills, Purchasing. Project Task Team: Robin Little, Leader; Kelly Reed; Marty Hanson; Sandy Saunders.

Schedule:
9:00   Introduction (Lee Smith)
9:05   Proposed Design Modifications (Robin Little)
9:20   Variation from current design (Kelly Reed)
9:30   Customer implications (Marty Hanson)
9:45   Discussion, consensus formation (Lee Smith)
10:50   Meeting evaluation (Lee Smith)
11:00   Adjournment

Enclosure: Copy of task team report. Please read this report and come to the meeting prepared to discuss it and make a decision.

Helpful Hint

Make up a form for the agenda of routine meetings to save time and keep the format consistent. This form should have space for time, place, objectives, attendees, assignments, etc. It can be a master form to be photocopied and filled in by hand, or it may be a computer template available on your word-processing program. There are even software programs available to help plan, organize and conduct meetings efficiently (see page 213).

Special Agenda Considerations

In addition to the basic information required in drafting an agenda, there are other issues to be addressed. The suggestions below will help you draft an agenda that addresses issues such as motivation and recognition while ensuring that you are including the right content and the right people:

- **Solicit Input**
  Meeting Masters avoid surprises by talking to people ahead of time (see page 26). Find out what people want to discuss and how they want to be involved. Then accommodate those requests as much as possible. When you are not able to include an item, or involve individuals in the way requested, let them know the reason why ahead of time.

- **Share the Credit**
  When somebody contributes an agenda item, don't hide its origin. Some people don't care, but others have personal reasons for wanting recognition of their idea. Passing it off as the leader's idea will discourage these people from submitting items ahead of time and provoke disruptive, spontaneous requests during the meeting.

- **Load the List**
  Put the most compelling items at the top. People will be fresher and better able to give their full attention. This will also encourage people to arrive on time.

- **Be Flexible**
  Consider special time constraints. Some individuals may not be needed for, or able to attend, the whole meeting. Arrange the agenda to coincide with their availability, and cluster items that involve them.

- **Consider Guests**
  Scheduling input from outsiders at the beginning of the meeting allows them to leave when they are finished. This will increase their willingness to attend future meetings when requested. It also allows you to conduct the rest of the meeting in privacy.

- **Vary the Format**
  Not every meeting requires a formal, lengthy agenda. Complicated meetings with lots of items and many people will benefit from an elaborate, formal agenda. More simple needs can be adequately addressed with memos.

Helpful Hint

When a long list of agenda items will be considered, only a small core of people needs to be involved with every item. In such cases, schedule people to attend only for those items for which their input or attention is important. This streamlines the process and makes the most efficient use of everyone's time.

Don't Forget the Donuts

Attention to seemingly small details can make the difference between a dull, unproductive meeting and one that is upbeat, enthusiastic, and really gets results. In general, these details concern equipment or supplies needed to perform the work of the meeting, and some of the "extras" that make people feel good about being there. Your special touches should be tailored to the nature of the meeting and the people who are attending. Examples of small details that can pay big dividends are listed below:

● **Donuts**
Sharing food is one of the oldest ways of building bonds between people. Donuts are classic meeting food. Even if they are on a diet, people's eyes light up when they spot a tray of donuts. They may not take one, but donuts are comfort food, and meetings are a good excuse to indulge. You can include a few bagels, bran muffins, or other appropriate refreshments for those with diet problems or different tastes. In the afternoon, cookies, cheese and crackers, or a vegetable tray are a tasty alternative.

● **Beverage**
For meetings lasting more than an hour, pitchers of water will keep people comfortable and reduce the need for frequent breaks. Coffee, tea, juice, or soda pop are welcome additions.

● **Flip Chart**
This is mandatory if you are doing brainstorming. It also comes in handy for other, often unexpected, purposes. Use pages from the pad for idea, agenda, and other bins (see page 88).

● **Note Pads, Pencils, etc.**
Imprinted items like pens, pencils, and note pads serve a double purpose. They are useful during the meeting, and keep your name in front of visitors later. For in-house meetings, supply any items like Post-It™ notes, note cards, or other specialized idea generation tools that you plan to use during the meeting.

● **Prepared Name Tags, etc.**
Laser printed name tags or tent cards are a nice touch for meetings where people aren't acquainted. If you can't prepare them ahead, have blank name tags and a felt-tip marker.

Marathon Meetings

Some meetings require a full day or longer. Typically, these meetings involve a group task, like strategic planning or proposal writing, that requires concentrated and focused attention. Extended meetings may be planned with people who have traveled considerable distances. These marathon meetings require intense planning to make the best use of time without creating burn-out and overload in the process. Factors that need to be considered are discussed below:

● **Location**
Meetings that require concentrated attention are appropriately held off-site to avoid the interruptions and distractions of routine business. Off-site locations may also stimulate creative thinking. If your meeting will involve subcommittees or task groups, make sure you have break-out rooms or similar space available for them to work concurrently without distracting each other. For multi-day meetings, such as strategic planning, that require fresh perspective and creative thinking, a resort or conference center can provide a valuable change of pace.

● **Planning**
A carefully prepared agenda is especially critical for marathon meetings. The longer the meeting, the easier it is to get off-track. Take extra care to generate mutual agreement ahead of time on items to be addressed, approximate time-frames, objectives to be achieved, roles people are to fill, and all necessary preliminary preparation.

● **Scheduling**
Frequent breaks and activities should be scheduled to reduce stress and avoid overload. For planning and task-oriented team meetings, tension break tactics help keep people feeling fresh and focused (see page 104). If the meeting continues non-stop for two or more days, a few hours for special activities such as sports, tours, games or general loafing are also helpful.

● **Ground Rules**
If the group holding the meeting doesn't already have mandated ground rules, make sure there is agreement on issues like accepting phone calls, leaving the meeting, interruptions by staff, etc. Such disruptions are highly undesirable. If outside business simply can't wait, schedule breaks appropriately to allow people to meet their obligations without disrupting the meeting.

● **Food**
Have refreshments available at all times. Although some people always want coffee and donuts, alternatives including juice, fruit, bran muffins, cheese, etc., are preferred by others. If the group is to stay together for meals, move to a different room, and arrange for well-prepared, high-quality food. It is also important to make sure any special dietary needs are identified and accommodated ahead of time. Putting people with allergies, special diets, religious proscriptions, or even

strong dislikes in the position of not eating part of the meal, or having to whisper to the waitress, can really spoil an event for them and create awkwardness for everyone.

● **Facilitation**
Planning, problem-solving and other meetings that involve intense concentration and creativity will benefit from involving a facilitator from outside the group (see page 136).

● **Professional Assistance**
A professional meeting planner can save you a lot of money when you are using an off-site location with many meals involved (see page 213).

Helpful Hint

If you have allergies or other dietary restrictions, make sure the meeting coordinator is aware of your needs ahead of time to avoid awkwardness at mealtimes.

Make Sure They're Ready

People who aren't used to preparing for meetings may need a few extra nudges to convert them. You know all the excuses, "I didn't have time," "I didn't realize we'd be covering that," "I almost forgot the meeting was today," "They didn't get the information to me..." Use ground rules to generate long-term cooperation in preparing (see page 66). When you don't have ground rules, use the guidelines below to ensure that participants at your meetings are well-prepared and won't need to make excuses:

● **Adequate Notice**
Be sure to give plenty of advance notice. Three days is the suggested minimum lead time for distributing the agenda, but let the complexity of the situation be your guide.

● **Follow-Up**
Telephone attendees ahead of time if you have any doubt that they will attend and/or be prepared. Explain the importance of their role and what is expected of them.

● **Be Prepared**
Set an example by being well-prepared yourself. Examples of personal preparation include:

 – Arriving on time
 – Bringing all relevant information and necessary supplies
 – Having a concise, well-organized presentation when you are giving a report or promoting an idea
 – Proactively finding answers to anticipated questions.

● **Introductions**
Introductions set the tone for the meeting and individual presentations. At the beginning of the meeting, make sure everyone knows who the other participants are, and why they are included. You can make these introductions yourself as leader, or have participants introduce themselves.

Helpful Hint

To help a group of total strangers get acquainted and begin working together, use an ice-breaker type of introduction. For example, ask people to give their names and titles. Then ask them to add an additional piece of information that will provide the basis for conversation later. This information might emphasize their usefulness to the group, or help start the discussion to be pursued during the meeting. Examples include:

– What I like to do for relaxation when I'm not working myself to death for The Company is...

– One of the best ideas I ever had was...

– If there were one thing I had total control over and could change to improve customer service in The Company, it would be...

Meeting Planner Form

The Planner Form on the following two pages serves as a checklist to make certain that all aspects of planning a meeting are considered and addressed.

In addition to its use in planning, the completed form can be used to track your success in planning and conducting meetings that stick to the agenda. To use it for evaluation, compare your planner form with the meeting minutes and note where deviations occur.

Meeting Planner Form

Meeting Name:		Place:	
Date:		Time: (Start/Stop)	
Mission:			
Objective(s):			
Type of Meeting:		Chair:	
Recorder:		Time Keeper:	
Members to Attend:		Role:	Phone #:
1			
2			
3			
4			
5			
6			
7			
8			
Items to be Discussed:			Time:
1			
2			
3			
4			
5			
6			
7			
8			
9			
10			

To Do Before Meeting:	By Whom:	By When:

Meeting Notes:		

Items For Follow-Up:	By Whom:	By When:

4

Meeting Masters' Trusty Tactics

Tracy was really ready for the meeting. The agenda had gone out a week before the meeting. Everyone giving reports was prepared. Possible antagonists had been mollified in advance. The room was in order, and things got off to a great start. But soon after the meeting was called to order, somebody brought up an issue that wasn't on the agenda. A hot discussion ensued with "Windy" Warren totally dominating. By the time they got to the scheduled reports, tempers were frayed, people were restless, and the discussion was unexpectedly hostile. When two people left because the meeting was running overtime, all decisions had to be postponed until another meeting could be scheduled.

As this example shows, laying the groundwork through adequate preparation is not enough to guarantee the successful outcome of a meeting. Once the meeting begins, meeting leaders face a whole new set of challenges. They must make sure it gets off to a good start. Their responsibility includes ensuring that each person gets a fair chance to be heard and no one dominates or filibusters. They keep the discussion on track so the meeting ends on schedule. When differences of opinion or conflicts surface, leaders expedite a resolution. Obviously, many things can happen to derail the meeting process.

Running a meeting well is an art, not unlike the job of a talk show host. Both require tact, timing, good communication skills, a bit of showmanship, and sometimes courage. If you have planned diligently and laid the groundwork, there should be few surprises. People will know what to expect, and have their thoughts and questions well organized. But controversy may still arise, tempers may flare, and people may sometimes ramble on ad nauseam. Your assignment as leader is to maintain control and keep the process on course.

Principle #3:
Use meeting ground rules to maintain focus, respect, and order.

Part of the excitement for a Meeting Master is rising to the occasion when something unexpected does occur. It is uniquely satisfying to be able to successfully resolve a confrontation, avoid disruption of scheduled and important discussions, and help people on opposite sides of the table generate mutually agreeable decisions. Ground rules, explained in this section, help you do this gracefully. Other guidelines will help you get things off to a positive start, conduct the entire meeting with polish, ensure that plans are carried out, and, when necessary, exercise back seat leadership.

How to Lead a Meeting

The role of the leader is complex. He or she is responsible for setting the tone of the meeting, keeping the discussion on track, and making sure everyone has a fair chance to be heard. The leader is the one who summarizes relevant points and ties things together when the discussion jumps around between inter-related topics.

Filling the role of discussion leader requires strong facilitation skills. Many people may prefer to pass the baton to someone else to lead all or part of the discussion. Depending on circumstances, this person may be someone in the group who has a knack for leading discussions (see page 85). A trained facilitator from outside the group is another viable option (see page 137). When there are several topics on the agenda, it is appropriate to rotate discussion leadership among the people in charge of various agenda items. In this case, the overall meeting leader may serve as a sort of master of ceremonies, introducing the various segments and tying them together.

For most meetings, when advance preparation has been prepared, leadership is a fairly simple process. Unfortunately, there is no way to guarantee that everyone will be present and prepared and no surprises will arise. Keeping everyone pulling in the same direction can be a challenge when personal agendas clash or misunderstandings occur. The meeting leader must harness these extraneous forces and use their power to enhance the meeting, rather than allow them to derail it. Below are brief guidelines for building on preparation and leading a meeting smoothly:

- **Begin on Time**
  Starting late subtly diminishes your credibility and the importance of the meeting. It sends the message that it is okay to be late, and shows a lack of respect and appreciation for those who make the effort to arrive on time.

- **Create a Positive Climate**
  A positive climate is based on mutual respect among all people participating. Many factors are involved (see page 63). One of the most important ways to enhance respect is to establish ground rules (see page 66). Set or review ground rules and use them to ensure open, freely flowing discussion. Although invoking ground rules is a shared responsibility for everyone in attendance, enforcing them falls first to the meeting leader.

- **Use the Agenda**
  Restate the purpose of the meeting at the beginning, and review the agenda to get agreement on time allocations (see

page 90). Continually refer back to the agenda throughout the meeting to keep discussion centered on the stated
purpose and objectives.

● **Facilitate the Discussion**
Steer the discussion without dominating it. Many people,
especially managers and supervisors who lead meetings with
their subordinates, don't understand the importance of this
role. They don't realize that they could manage better if
they spoke less and listened more. They feel compelled to
restate and embellish every thought expressed by anyone in
the group. Their behavior sends messages that subordinates
can't express themselves clearly, and that there is only one
opinion that counts. In brief, such chronic restatement is
demeaning and demoralizing.

Discussion leaders should be objective, without passing
judgment or commenting at length on the ideas being
expressed (see page 86). Strategies like restating ideas and
asking questions are helpful to make sure everyone shares
understanding of the message. But, this clarification
should not run into lengthy dissertations.

Objectivity is always important, especially during
discussions. However, there are many times where opinions
of the meeting leader are relevant and expected. For example,
training meetings, meetings planned primarily to convey
information, or staff and other similar meetings are instances
where the manager or supervisor is expected to provide
opinions and guidance.

Guidelines for listening and using questions effectively
will help both discussion leaders and participants (see pages
119-122).

● **Stay on Track**
Tactfully discourage digressions and clarify or summarize
points as they are made.

- **Be Forthright**
  Confront underlying issues that cause conflict. Get them out in the open and clear them up.

- **Control Dominating Individuals**
  Make sure each person has a fair chance to express ideas and opinions without allowing any individual to dominate the discussion. Refer to the ground rules to tactfully cut short long-winded harangues (see page 66).

- **Monitor Nonverbal Signals**
  Seek input from quiet members who may be shy, or otherwise reluctant to voice reservations or disagreement with the ideas of others (see page 94).

Helpful Hint

Many meeting leaders find it helpful to appoint a monitor to watch for nonverbal signals that the communication process may need some attention, or that the group is losing sight of the task at hand. Some leaders are adept at remaining aware of both task-oriented interaction and group process. Others are stronger at one or the other. Some are strong at both, but intense situations call for assistance (see page 41). A wise leader knows his or her limits, and arranges for appropriate backup.

An effective monitor interjects observations as appropriate. For example, a monitor observing group process may notice that a member, Fred, has ceased to participate actively and appears withdrawn. The monitor will cut into the discussion at an appropriate point with a question such as, "Fred, you look thoughtful. Could you share your thoughts on (the matter under discussion)?"

When the monitor is tracking task-oriented discussion, referring items to the Idea Bin is a good way to get the discussion back on track (see page 89).

- **Summarize**
  Conclude the meeting by summarizing the discussion, decisions made, and tasks delegated; then review plans for follow-up. Review or set the time for any succeeding meetings.

- **End on Time**

Leadership Styles

The leadership style of the person conducting the meeting strongly influences both the meeting process and the ability of the group to produce effective results. Studying leadership styles can teach you new techniques to improve the results of groups you lead. This study may include reading books and articles, attending workshops, finding a mentor, and observing the techniques and behavior of other successful leaders.

Three commonly discussed leadership styles are described in the following table, along with a fourth, which is currently gaining recognition.

Type	AKA	Attributes	Typical Outcomes
Minimalist	Laissez-faire	Lets group run itself with little inter-vention. Generally lacks structure and focus.	Rambling discussion, confusion, few decisions. Eventual apathy, stagnation, disintegration of group. *Exceptions: Self-directed groups with high cohesion.*

Type	AKA	Attributes	Typical Outcomes
Dictator	Autocratic	High degree of control over everything: planning, discussion, decisions.	Lack of commitment to decisions. Anger, frustration, avoidance of meetings. *Exceptions: Crisis situation, highly respected leader.*
Facilitator	Participative	Highly participative style with input solicited from all group members before decisions are made. Heavy reliance on majority rule.	General enthusiasm and support, high involvement and productivity. *Exceptions: Indecisive leader who defers decisions.*
Consensus Builder	No alternate term identified	Ultimate form of participative leadership. Heavy reliance on consensus form of decision-making.	High degree of commitment to decisions, and strong support for implementation and follow-through.

Meeting Climate

Everyone has attended meetings that constantly digressed onto side issues and jumped back and forth between agenda items. Jumping around is disconcerting to most people, and it is even worse when conflict is involved. Meetings that consistently bounce from one topic to another lack focus and seldom achieve their objectives.

In addition to careful planning and choosing the right setting (see page 35), these problems can be overcome by taking a few minutes at the start of the meeting to establish a positive climate. Besides social amenities, this involves agreeing on ground rules, just as you would for a game of tennis or soccer, and reviewing the purpose of the meeting. This process focuses attention on the meeting topics, and sets the tone for the ensuing discussion.

The following guidelines will help get the meeting off to a successful start:

- **Check Things Out**
  Be sure someone arrives early enough to check setup details and take care of any last minute snafus.

- **Be a Good Host**
  Chat informally with attendees as they arrive.

- **Make Introductions**
  If people haven't already met everyone, or if the role of people in the meeting isn't clear, conduct introductions at the beginning, including the reason each is attending. If there are more than two or three strangers, provide name tags as a courtesy to those who have trouble remembering names.

- **Be Positive**
  Begin the meeting on a positive note, not by groaning about complications or problems preceding the meeting.

- **Review the Agenda**
  Make sure everyone understands the expectations and objectives for the meeting.

- **Set Ground Rules**
  Review or introduce guidelines for structuring the discussion. These rules may include time limits, limits on the number

of times an individual may speak about each issue, etc. (see page 66).

- **Be Organized**
  Set an example for others by being personally prepared and having all necessary papers, supplies and other items readily accessible.

Process Pavers

Meeting Masters, whether in the leadership chair or not, share certain characteristics that contribute to their positive impact during meetings. These characteristics are demonstrated by the way they respond to new ideas, interact with other people, and express disagreement.

Their most important characteristics are summarized below:

- **Objectivity**
  Meeting Masters' ability to evaluate an idea on its own merits, without jumping to conclusions, contributes to the open and free-flowing discussion that is critical to effective meetings. They are quick to confront assumptions and conclusions based on shaky evidence or emotion, but they do so in a non-threatening way. They use a lot of questions and support their positions with logic as strongly as possible. (see page 121).

- **Spontaneity**
  Meetings are more productive when there is enough trust and acceptance for members to speak their minds freely. The discussion process is seriously stifled when people must have undue concern about the literal meaning or political correctness of every word they utter. The directness, objectivity, and spontaneity of Meeting Masters contributes to the

development of this trust. They also use ground rules about confidentiality and establishing the desirability of spontaneous expression (see below).

- **Empathy**
  The awareness and sensitivity of Meeting Masters to the feelings of other participants lubricates the process and allows the free flow of ideas.

- **Respect**
  Meeting Masters diligently allow others the right to express differing opinions, the right to be thoughtfully listened to, the right to speak without being interrupted, and the right to be treated with dignity.

- **Focus**
  Meeting Masters demonstrate self-discipline by sticking to the subject and avoiding the temptation to tell long, humorous stories. They avoid the distraction of emotional tirades and unrelated side issues, and they keep personal notes on ideas that need to be brought up in the future.

- **Humility**
  Although they often emanate a certain charisma, Meeting Masters shy away from pedestals. Their behavior minimizes inequality and deference within the group.

Suggested Ground Rules

Not so long ago, any proper meeting at which business was conducted was run by parliamentary procedure, as specifically defined by the classic work *Robert's Rules Of Order*. Veteran meeting leaders had most of this book committed to memory, but packed a well-worn copy along to meetings, just in case it was needed as a reference tool.

Mr. Robert's rules are still in order, but no longer in widespread use. In today's participative climate, free-flowing discussion and consensus often replaces formal motions, debates and votes. This is partly due to the structure of parliamentary procedure, which does not lend itself well to the give-and-take so vital for arriving at consensus. Furthermore, the Rules break down when meetings are called for purposes such as brainstorming, resolving problems, or presenting information. In short, they don't address the needs of many contemporary meeting formats.

Unfortunately, no clearly defined protocol has arisen to replace or expand this time-honored tradition. This void often creates dilemmas and saps the productivity and effectiveness of meetings. Without an articulated set of rules, each person arrives at a meeting with personal expectations about "the way things should be done at meetings." When these expectations clash, the process suffers. The lack of standards makes the resulting conflict harder to resolve. This lack also makes it difficult to control productivity drains, such as long-winded participants, people who are chronically late, or people who take phone calls during the meeting. They can't be confronted with a breach of the rules when there aren't any rules!

Meeting Masters are unanimous in advocating the adoption of *group generated* ground rules that cover the specific needs and situations faced by any group that frequently meets together. The group formulates the ground rules by consensus, as procedural guidelines. As the composition of the group changes over time, new members are provided with a copy to help them participate smoothly and effectively from the beginning.

Ground rules are not as rigid as they might sound. If any particular item begins to chafe, and is frequently broken, the group can change it. The rules are made to facilitate group interaction, not to restrict it.

In temporary or one-time meeting groups, it is helpful for the leader to suggest simple ground rules at the beginning of the meeting. This gives those present the opportunity to discuss and modify them before agreeing to abide by them. When the meeting will be formal or highly structured, it is helpful to incorporate a definition of ground rules into the agenda under the heading of "procedure."

Suggested elements for workable ground rules are listed below, with an explanation of each. Use them as a starting point to formulate ground rules that reflect your group's specific situation.

- **Purpose**
  State the purpose of the meeting or the mission of an on-going group. For example, "The purpose of our group is to identify effective strategies for improving customer service in the Eastern Division and to make recommendations on implementation of these strategies." If you aren't clear on the purpose or mission of the group, you won't make much progress in achieving tangible results. Schedule some meeting time to clarify what it is you are trying to do. Relate that the meeting leader's function is to facilitate discussion and keep order within the group.

- **Personal Responsibility**
  Define areas of personal responsibility, i.e., "We will speak only for ourselves. Terms such as 'everyone,' 'lots of people,' or 'we/they/all' are to be avoided."

- **Mutual Respect**
  Provide a way of resolving disagreements and similar situations, i.e., "We will respect the rights of all present to be heard and to receive fair consideration. We will avoid interruptions, personal criticism, and other disrespectful treatment."

- **Clarity**
  Define a way to discourage rambling and domination of the meeting, i.e., "We will provide feedback to each other during the evaluation period to increase our ability to express ourselves clearly and concisely."

- **Focus**
  Give collective responsibility for keeping the meeting on track, i.e., "When anyone begins to ramble, it is our collective responsibility to refocus the discussion on the agenda and bring it back to task."

- **Control**
  Define any strategies to be used for maintaining control of meeting time, i.e., "We will use a time-keeper when needed to keep presentations on schedule." (see page 92).

Other guidelines will suggest themselves as your group evolves and grows in experience and maturity. Remember, this is a process and, like any process, it will benefit from continuous evaluation and improvement. Periodically review and update the ground rules to keep the meeting climate healthy.

Sample Ground Rules

The sample ground rules listed below were drawn up by a cross-functional corporate project review team that meets once a month. This long form of the rules is signed by the members and kept for reference. The action-oriented summary is posted in the room and pointed out at the beginning of each meeting to keep the rules firmly in everyone's mind (see page 74).

The list is fairly new. Two new rules have been added since the original list was formulated, and additional rules may be added as time goes by.

1. **Schedule**
   Meetings will begin promptly at 3:40 p.m. on the first business Monday of each month. We will end promptly at 5 p.m. In extenuating circumstances, we may agree by consensus to extend the meeting time.

2. **Be on Time**
    We will arrive at least five minutes early in order to be
    settled and ready to work at the appointed time.

3. **Attendance**
    Attendance is a top priority for all of us. If we have an
    unavoidable conflict, such as being out of town, we will
    notify the meeting leader as soon as possible. Even when
    we are absent, we are responsible for ensuring that our
    responsibilities are carried out and a report is available in
    our absence.

4. **Preparation**
    We will each be familiar with items on the agenda before we
    arrive and be prepared for our individual assignments. We
    will provide presenters with as many questions as possible
    ahead of time to assist them in their preparation and save
    time in obtaining answers.

5. **Leadership**
    The meeting leader will be responsible for facilitating
    discussion, ensuring that we stay on track with the topic
    under discussion, and that each member has, and takes
    advantage of, the opportunity to participate. The meeting
    leader will be the chief facilitator for resolving conflict or
    differences of opinion, but any member is welcome to assist
    in this process.

6. **Procedure**
    We will begin each meeting with the following steps:

    a. A review of our Mission Statement.

    b. Summary and acceptance of minutes of the previous
        meeting.

c. Review of the agenda and agreement on order and time
    allocation for agenda items. From that point on, we will
    stick to the agreed upon order and time limits.

d. Update on actions taken since last meeting.

7. **Idea Jar**
    We will write down spontaneous ideas pertaining to items
    further down the agenda and save them for the appropriate
    time. Ideas pertaining to items we have already discussed
    will be written on a memo slip and put in the Idea Jar,
    which will be kept in the center of the table (see page 89).
    These slips will be reviewed at the end of the meeting.

8. **Participation**
    We will listen respectfully, without interruption or side
    conversations. If one person begins to dominate or ramble,
    members of the group share responsibility for pointing
    out this behavior. Members who are having difficulty
    getting a turn to speak will signal their desire to speak
    with raised hands. This signal will be acknowledged by the
    meeting leader.

9. **Disruptions**
    No disruptions such as phone calls or other messages from
    outside the room will be allowed. No one will leave the
    meeting for anything other than a group-related task or
    health-related needs.

10. **Conflict Resolution**
    We recognize conflict and difference of opinion as a valuable
    resource to be used for constructive purposes. All conflict
    and differences of opinion will be approached with open
    minds and the intent of identifying win/win resolutions.

11. **Meeting Climate**

We want to maintain a positive atmosphere within the meeting and will avoid the use of killer phrases (see page 105). Members who use killer phrases (demeaning, derogatory or persistently negative comments) will have a small sandbag placed on the table in front of them. Four such bags will be kept in the supply kit with the markers, name tags and other supplies for our meetings. Any member is free to take one of the bags and place it quietly in front of the negative member. No comment is necessary, but the action may be discussed then or later if anyone brings it up. The sandbag should be awarded immediately for demeaning or derogatory remarks. Negative comments may be ignored until three or four have established a pattern.

Negative comments are defined as general statements such as "That would never work," "I don't know why we can never...," or "I don't know why we bother..." Objective observation of problems or weaknesses in proposed ideas is not considered negative comments.

12. **Humor**

Even though our business is serious, we believe that *conducting it should be fun*. Appropriate humor is encouraged at all times within the following guidelines:

a. It should be short and to the point.

b. We will not get into prolonged story-swapping sessions during meeting time.

c. No humorous remark will be acceptable if it is demeaning or hurtful to others. This includes jokes and comments with a racial, ethnic, sexual, violent or similar theme.

13. Decisions

We will use consensus as our primary decision-making tool. The meeting leader or a designated alternate will facilitate the formation of consensus. Responsibility for specific decisions may be delegated to individuals or committees by group consensus.

14. Delegation

Assignments for follow-up tasks identified during the meeting will held in the Assignments Jar and assigned near the end of the meeting (see page 89). This will distribute the load more equitably, and prevent anyone from prematurely volunteering for a task that would preclude their acceptance of a more relevant one later.

15. Evaluation

We will schedule seven minutes on the agenda at the end of each meeting to evaluate the meeting's productivity and the quality of the process. The attached standard form will be used for this purpose (see form on page 111).

16. Ground Rule Review

These ground rules are subject to negotiation, addition or subtraction by group consensus. They are to be reviewed at the March meeting each year, but any member may request the addition or review of individual items at any time.

All members, present and future, will sign a copy of the ground rules for the file, and receive a copy for their own reference. It is our collective responsibility to follow and enforce these ground rules for our mutual benefit.

> ### *Helpful Hint*
>
> The sandbags described in these ground rules are small, colorful bags of fabric (made by a member), approximately 3"x 5", and loosely filled with coarse sand. Beans, rice, or a similar substance would also make an appropriate filling.

Ground Rules, Short Form

1. Arrive and start on time.
2. Be there.
3. Be prepared.
4. Share responsibility for following and enforcing the ground rules.
5. Stick to the agenda.
6. Listen respectfully and thoughtfully.
7. No interruptions, side conversations, phone calls, or other disruptions.
8. No silent observers.
9. No killer phrases.
10. Have fun with appropriate humor.
11. Use consensus to make major decisions.
12. Be realistic when accepting responsibility for follow-up tasks.

(These ground rules are displayed during each meeting by the group that drafted them.)

Tips for Constructing Ground Rules

Constructing a set of ground rules can be threatening because it involves talking about problems. The problems that are identified, i.e., tardiness, dominating the discussion, or interruptions, generally reflect the behavior of one or more individuals. These people may become defensive and can construe the discussion as a personal attack. The key to keeping the process constructive lies in depersonalizing the issues. Focus on *what* is wrong, not *who* is wrong. Then state the desired outcome. For example, if tardiness is a problem, it can be stated that, "We are wasting a lot of time repeating things for latecomers, and sometimes things get left out. This makes it hard to make good decisions. Our meetings will be more productive if we all arrive on time."

Most groups benefit from the process of developing ground rules internally. However, if ground rules are being developed for collective use by a number of groups, or other complicating factors are involved, you can save time and get better results by seeking assistance from a meeting coach (see page 77).

The tips below will help you maintain a low-key, objective, non-threatening atmosphere during the formulation process:

- **Take it Easy**
  The length of time required to formulate ground rules depends on the complexity of your requirements. If your meetings are short and simple, your ground rules don't need to be elaborate. If you conduct long involved meetings that require addressing many process problems, allow some time. Don't try to formulate and adopt a complete set of ground rules during one meeting. Allow two or three sessions to give people time to think things over.

- **Identify Problems**
  Have the group brainstorm things that are impairing group productivity. Phrase input in terms of behavior, with no reference to specific personalities. This is an excellent time to use written input, which can be prepared and collected between meetings. Use 3"x 5" cards and write only one idea per card.

- **Sort Input**
  If input was generated as lists, transfer ideas to 3"x 5" cards, as described above. Sort the cards into groups of related ideas, such as starting on time, communication problems, etc.

- **Define Desired Behavior and Conditions**
  These will be *your* ground rules. Simply state the way you want things to be, for example, "Meetings will begin at the stated time, whether or not all participants are present." Or, "Participants will arrive at least five minutes before the stated meeting time in order to be ready to start on time." Keep the focus on behavior (i.e., "participants will arrive...") and conditions (i.e., "whether or not all participants are present"), so that the rules can be invoked objectively.

- **Use Consensus**
  Get consensus from the group for each item (see page 142). If a ground rule is proposed and someone has a problem with it, ask, "How can we change it so you can be comfortable with it?"

- **Distribute Completed Ground Rules**
  Have each member of the group sign a master copy for dramatic impact, and keep this copy on file. Give each participant a copy for personal reference.

- **Use Them**
  Ground rules do you no good at all if you don't use them. If infractions are interfering with the process, i.e., talking too long, bring them up at the time. Others, like late arrivals, can be discussed during the evaluation period at the end of the meeting.

Help with Ground Rules

The guidelines and instructions provided on the preceding pages tell you everything you need to know to formulate effective ground rules. Working through the process on your own is a good idea. It increases the commitment and motivation of the group to use them. However, sometimes it saves considerable time, and possibly grief, to call in a meeting coach. Most of the reasons for using an external meeting coach are the same as the reasons for using external facilitators (see page 137).

It can be challenging to find a coach who fully understands the concept of ground rules. Many management consultants offer meeting improvement services, but few know about this approach. If you know a consultant who has provided satisfactory service on other projects, share the material in this handbook. If the person readily accepts your proposed course of action, the project should have a good outcome. Don't let yourself be bullied into accepting other solutions. Unless you are convinced another approach is really better, keep looking for someone who will do things your way.

Examples of situations where you will benefit from calling in a meeting coach are listed below:

● **Confusion About Strategies**
Sometimes it isn't clear what the problems are, or how to solve them. A certain amount of trial-and-error is healthy. However, you can save valuable time and often get better results by asking for help from an experienced coach.

● **Dominating Individuals**
Groups that include people who dominate discussions and/or intimidate others face extra problems. This situation makes it especially difficult to develop strategies to control the behavior causing the problem. This is especially true if the dominating individual just happens to be the boss! Many people are intimidated by anyone in a position of authority. Using a coach can neutralize this effect.

- **Passive Participants**
  Some people are slow to respond and discuss anything.
  Others are reluctant to participate in discussions that may
  generate conflict or cause hurt feelings. Still others may feel
  intimidated by authority, as discussed above. This lack of
  candor sabotages the formulation of ground rules as well as
  other decisions. Coaching specialists have strategies for getting
  everyone involved.

- **Gridlock**
  Now and then a group may be unable to reach consensus
  on recommended solutions. Coaches can help you generate
  additional alternatives that are better than anything you
  disagreed about.

Meeting Minutes

A formal record of meetings may be required by the charter or
by-laws of formally constituted, on-going groups, like task
forces or boards of directors. Less formal meetings will also benefit
from keeping meeting minutes. This record serves several purposes.
It provides continuity, serves as a resource for resolving conflicting
memories, keeps absent members up-to-date, aids in accountability,
and provides historical documentation.
　　Follow these hints to use minutes effectively:

- **Recorder**
  Select an organized, articulate person to be responsible for
  the minutes when there is no officially mandated secretary
  or recorder.

- **Distribution**
  When detailed, or longer than one page, mail minutes to
  members before the next meeting. You can include them
  with the agenda and other preparation material for the
  next meeting.

- **Approval**
  Read minutes of the previous meeting at the beginning of the current one. If they were distributed earlier, a summary will do. Call for additions or corrections before approving them.

- **Continuity**
  Note items from the minutes that are included on the current agenda. This provides continuity and long-range focus for the group.

- **Personal Notes**
  Members will benefit from keeping their own notes, particularly when they are responsible for actions to be taken between meetings. Furthermore, personal notes occasionally include insights and information not included in the formal minutes, and provide a valuable resource for making additions or corrections to the minutes.

  Several Meeting Masters recommend keeping notes in your Day-Timer® or other personal organizer system. This is especially useful when you delegate assignments. People are far more likely to take the deadline seriously if they notice you making a note of the follow-up date on your calendar. The same system will help keep you on track with your own obligations.

How to Take Minutes

Literal transcripts of meetings are rarely required. If you should ever be in such a situation, use a tape recorder! Under normal circumstances, the scope and depth of the minutes will be determined by a combination of group needs and the note-taking style of the designated recorder.

The purpose of minutes is to ensure clarification and shared understanding among those attending, to provide a running record of decisions and how they were reached, and to remind those involved of projects underway before the next meeting. Effective minutes should include the following:

- **Date, Time, and Place**

- **Attendance List**
  List all attendees, along with their titles or other identifying information when relevant.

- **Agenda Items**
  Include a brief summary of the discussion for each item with names of key contributors.

- **Motions**
  Record all motions and their subsequent disposal along with the names of people making and seconding each. Make note of any amendments and relevant discussion.

- **Decisions**
  Include definition of problems identified and considered, with alternatives presented for each item and solutions agreed upon.

- **Assignments**
  Make note of all assignments made and accepted, with agreed-upon deadlines and follow-up actions to be taken.

Meeting Minutes Form

For routine meetings with a relatively standard format, there are many advantages to using a standardized form for taking minutes. The form simplifies the job of the recorder, and standardizes the minutes from one meeting to the next. For example, it ensures that standard information such as the time spent in the meeting and those attending is recorded. Assuming that the recorder has reasonably legible penmanship, the form can simply be copied and distributed to all concerned immediately after the meeting, eliminating the need for anyone to type up the minutes.

A sample form is printed on the following two pages. You can use it as a guideline for designing your own, allowing as much space as desired for each item. The boxes labeled "Item #" are provided to record discussion about individual agenda items. Only Item #1 is numbered. Subsequently, space is provided to record the number of the item being discussed. Use as many copies of the second sheet as necessary to cover all items. Extra spaces should be available for additional items that come up during the meeting. A copy of the agenda should be attached to the Minutes Form for identification of the items.

In designing your own form, you may want to add space at the end for recording items for later discussion and follow-up that are placed in bins (see page 88).

To use this form, condense and summarize the discussion, including only the main points. Use the Decision box to record the decision reached, even if it was to delay further discussion until a future time. In the Follow-up box, record dates for future action, along with names and specific responsibilities for delegated tasks.

The form is best suited for meetings where many items are being discussed, and discussion of each is relatively short. If you have one or two items where discussion is more involved, add extra pages of blank paper to continue the record. This form is not appropriate for situations where a detailed log of the discussion is necessary, or occasions when you need to keep track of who said what.

Meeting Minutes Form

Meeting Name:		
Date:	Place:	
Start:	Stop:	Total:
Attending: (list all)		
Absent: (list all)		
Roles: (list all)		
Item #1: Discussion		
Decision:		
Follow-up:		

Item #   : Discussion

Decision:

Follow-up:

Item #   : Discussion

Decision:

Follow-up:

Late Arrivals

Timely arrival is standard operating procedure for responsible professionals. There are legitimate reasons for being late, but regardless of the reason, late arrivals can be disruptive. It is important to handle them as smoothly and quietly as possible. This avoids embarrassment for some latecomers, and lessens the likelihood of distracting grand entrances by others. Use appropriate preparation tactics to discourage chronic or careless late arrivals (see pages 35, 48, and 59).

These guidelines will help you handle latecomers deftly during the meeting:

- **Ignore Them**
  When latecomers enter discreetly and quietly take a seat, continue the meeting without making mention of their arrival.

- **Point Out a Seat**
  If latecomers stand in the door, look confused, etc., invite them to take a seat, then continue without further interruption.

- **Minimize Interaction**
  If a latecomer does disrupt the group, steer the group back to the agenda and current topic of discussion as quickly as possible. Generally speaking, no attempt should be made to bring the latecomer up-to-speed, as this further disrupts the meeting and reduces incentive to be on time in the future.

- **Be Flexible**
  If others have been worried about the reason for the tardiness of the latecomer, or if there is some other compelling reason for interrupting the proceedings, do what you have to do, and then get back to the discussion.

How to Lead a Discussion

Whether you chair meetings or just participate, it helps to develop a knack for leading discussions well. This is not a complicated process. As the discussion leader, it is your job to objectively manage the flow of ideas rather than contribute much of your own thinking. Your job is to help generate shared understanding about the topic of discussion. If you have strong ideas on the subject and a lot to say, it is better to request that someone else lead the discussion.

Guidelines for leading a discussion follow:

- **Enforce the Agenda**
  A well-planned agenda is a big help in leading the discussion, because it defines the objectives and defines time guidelines. Refer to the objectives and discussion deadline as necessary to keep the discussion on track. If you must lead a discussion in a meeting with no agenda, be resourceful. Clarify the objectives and timing with the meeting chair and the rest of the group before beginning the discussion.

- **Incorporate the Ground Rules**
  Ground rules are made to be used, so use them. If the group lacks formal ground rules, set some ad hoc ones. Make a simple statement of expectations to help limit long-winded speakers. For example, you may say, "I'm sure you all have a lot to say, and to make sure everyone gets a fair turn, let's limit remarks to a maximum of two minutes per turn." With these few words you have set a couple of ad hoc ground rules and gained control.

- **Ensure that All Views are Heard**
  Use the ground rules to make sure that nobody dominates the discussion, and that all have a chance to state their views. Be alert for anyone who seems reluctant to participate. Ask these people specific questions to encourage

involvement. This step is especially important when you are forming consensus.

● **Keep the Discussion on Track**
When speakers begin to ramble, or the discussion jumps to another topic, intervene as soon as possible. Make note of the digression, using bins or any other selected strategy, to keep the idea from being lost (see page 88). Then remind the group of the discussion objectives and allow it to proceed.

● **Clarify and Summarize Ideas**
Take time periodically to review the concepts covered. Simply restate the ideas and ask for the speaker's concurrence on accuracy. This is a big help in keeping the discussion on track and increasing the likelihood that shared understanding is developing. At the conclusion of the discussion, review the whole process. Ask for any necessary decisions, and schedule appropriate follow-up.

Keeping the Discussion on Track

In spite of everyone's best intentions and efforts, discussions often ramble. The best way to deal with the problem is to address it in ground rules (see page 66). If the group has agreed to keep the discussion on track, it is easy for anyone to simply observe, "Hey, we're really starting to stray." Everyone understands what this means and can quickly refocus.

Groups with a long history of rambling may need some extra help, at least for awhile. The following tested techniques can be incorporated into ground rules and will keep things moving. None require using a time-keeper. In each case, the group should acknowledge the need before using the technique. Agree ahead of time to recognize the signal, then use it consistently.

- **Nonverbal Signals**
  Overt signals, such as a raised index finger, provide a low-key way for the group to enforce ground rules. If these signals aren't defined, they won't be understood.

  Other common tactics, like avoiding eye contact, leaning back in your chair, or leafing through papers, may stop rambling speakers, but only when they are noticed. Even when it works, such behavior is demeaning and may make the speaker feel foolish, angry, and vengeful. None of these behaviors fosters group harmony.

- **Broken Record**
  An old, well-battered phonograph record, is placed in the center of the table at the beginning of the meeting. The record is quietly positioned in front of any speaker who strays from the stated objectives and/or begins to repeat or overstate things.

  Other suitable objects include something like a zipper or a tube of lip balm signifying "mouth care."

- **Thoughtful Interruption**
  Interrupting is never the tactic of first choice. But in a meeting with loose leadership, no ground rules, no defined time guidelines, and people who have trouble getting to the point, it may be expedient. The least offensive way to interrupt is to raise a finger, or stand up and ask for permission to make a point. Then keep talking. Be sure you keep your own point short, sweet and simple!

  Since interrupting is incompatible with an atmosphere of free-flowing communication, limit its use to the legitimate function of cutting off digressions and overstatement of issues.

Hold that Thought

Insisting on following the agenda poses the potential dilemma of losing genuinely valuable ideas that don't relate to the current topic. These ideas are easily lost if they aren't immediately verbalized. The solution is to use some mechanism for storing, sorting and considering these ideas at appropriate and convenient times.

Several Meeting Masters use "bins" for this purpose. These bins consist of blank sheets torn from a flip chart and taped to the wall. Members are each provided with pads of Post-It™ notes. Any idea that is unrelated to the current topic is written on one of these notes and posted on the appropriate bin sheet. Some bins are designated for keeping track of issues: items or ideas that come up in discussion and need to be kept for later action. Notes in each bin are reviewed at the end of the meeting (if time is short, most of the bins can be put off for a later time) and discussed, delegated, or delayed for further action.

You don't have to cover your walls with paper to use this idea, and you don't need a warehouse to store equipment for meetings. Jars, boxes, or other receptacles can be positioned on the table and used to collect memo slips. These slips can be stored in file folders or envelopes between meetings. Whatever the collection method, use the following categories as guidelines for developing your own system:

- **Agenda Items Bin**
  This is the place to keep items that need to be scheduled on the agenda of a future meeting for follow-up or other action. Always check this bin at the end of the meeting while you are drafting the agenda for the next meeting.

- **Action Items Bin**
  Items requiring follow-up action are kept here. Deferring assignments until the end of the meeting allows you to look at the overall picture. Each person can then accept or volunteer for tasks that make best use of their talents and available time.

- **Decisions Bin**

  When you have many decisions that need to be delayed until some future time, keep track of them with a decisions bin. Designate someone in the group to make a tickler file from the slips in this bin. This will remind you to follow-up on each one at the appropriate time.

- **Ideas Bin**

  This is an all-purpose bin for new ideas someone wants to have considered at an appropriate time.

- **Synergism Bin**

  When someone has an idea that builds on a current issue, it goes into the synergism bin. Some ideas will be sparked that fall under the jurisdiction of people or groups outside the one holding the meeting. These should also go into the synergism bin. When it is reviewed, these outside suggestions are delegated to someone from the meeting group who will then follow-up with the appropriate people.

How to Control Meeting Time

Well-planned, well-run meetings generate a sense of satisfaction among attendees. They increase effectiveness and productivity, and they are an excellent investment of time. Unfortunately, some meetings tend to drag on far too long, becoming a major source of wasted time. The cost of the waste is compounded by the number of people involved. Much of this waste can be prevented by circulating a thoughtfully constructed agenda in time for attendees to prepare for the meeting. But all this planning is out-the-window if the meeting process runs out of control.

The following tips will help everyone keep the meeting on track and on schedule:

- **Negotiate Time Allocations**
  A good way to get the group to stick to the agenda and abide by time limits is to take three or four minutes at the beginning of the meeting to review the agenda. Ask them to suggest changes if they think some items will require more time. Of course, to gain that time, they have to be willing to give up time elsewhere or prolong the meeting. Group decisions about timing are virtually self-enforcing.

- **Stick to the Subject**
  Keep the focus sharp. Don't allow the discussion to ramble onto side issues or unrelated discussion. This will be a special challenge in meetings that include highly creative, visionary people. They see relationships between nearly all topics and tend to jump around between topics. Although their nonlinear thinking may be disconcerting, their observations often have considerable relevance and merit. When creativity is important, adjust the definition of relevance accordingly to avoid losing the benefit of their insight. Using an Ideas Bin is one way to help creative people hold onto their thoughts and ideas without being disruptive (see page 89).

- **Keep it Simple**
  Avoid overstatement and repetition of ideas.

- **Use Time Limits**
  Make sure you have ground rules with time limits and refer to them as necessary to keep the discussion relevant.

- **Avoid Surprises**
  Don't expand the agenda with spontaneous items. Save them for a future meeting, deal with them another way, or schedule a few minutes at the end for unexpected topics.

- **Stop on Time**
  Announce this intention at the beginning of the meeting
  and stick to it.

- **Be Flexible**
  When genuine confusion needs to be cleared up, or when serious
  differences of opinion must be resolved, you may need more
  time than you expected. When the meeting obviously will be
  prolonged more than a few minutes beyond the scheduled
  ending time, consider these options: get agreement from
  the group to prolong the meeting, allow uninvolved people
  to leave, or table the remaining business for a follow-up
  session to be held as soon as possible.

The Clock is Running

Setting time limits for meetings has both benefits and
disadvantages. Consider the purpose of the meeting and nature
of agenda items when making decisions about time limits. For
example, when the meeting agenda includes consensus formation,
allow ample time, because reaching consensus can become an
agonizingly slow process (see page 142). Rigid time constraints
may block the process completely when resolving differences of
opinion. Time limits may create pressure that causes grudging
compromise or capitulation on decisions, rather than concurrence.
These decisions, made by default, don't have a good record of
long-term success. Creativity and problem-solving also require
an unhurried atmosphere. Although nobody should be allowed
to ramble or dominate, it is important to make sure all views are
expressed. This takes ample time and patience.

The personality types of those attending are also an important
factor in planning time limits. Cautious, detail-oriented people
may need time to ask lots of questions and think over the
answers before making decisions or recommendations. Highly
sociable people will chafe under restrictions that draw too tight

a rein on their need to talk. Laid-back people don't care much one way or the other about time, but they don't like to be hurried. Driven personalities who over-schedule, over-commit, and tend to take charge, will find motor-mouths and people who ask seemingly redundant questions irritating. These personality differences are the source of a lot of conflict and exasperation. This is one major reason for a strong set of ground rules that are agreeable to everyone.

Given the above considerations, time limits are both appropriate and helpful. But they are only beneficial if they are put into action and enforced. Below are proven suggestions for helping the group stick to agreed-upon time limits:

● **Time-Keeper**
   Several types of meetings can benefit from the use of a formal time-keeper. Examples of situations when this would be useful include:

   – Meetings that involve input from a number of people on one or more issues.

   – Meetings where there is a lot of business to be attended to and time is short.

   – Meetings that involve one or more people known to be longwinded and dominating.

   – Meetings that involve public input.

   Your ground rules should establish whether you use a time-keeper in a regularly scheduled meeting. When time limits will be enforced during a formal meeting or hearing, any one making presentations should be alerted in advance.
   To use a timing system, appoint an official time-keeper, who will arrange signals with speakers to keep them on schedule. The time-keeper may also help limit less formal

discussion by signaling, as pre-defined or agreed upon by the group, at the end of the designated length of time allowed for each person to speak.

For time periods exceeding three minutes, the time-keeper should signal the speaker with some device, like upheld fingers, or green, yellow and red cards, to show the number of remaining minutes. Groups that routinely use a time-keeper may want to purchase a battery-operated signaling device, such as those sold by Toastmasters International (see page 213).

- **Merging Views**
  This technique is useful for managing the flow of discussion about a controversial topic. The discussion leader presents both sides of the issue. Participants then take turns speaking for and against the issue, alternating sides. A time limit may be agreed upon for each comment.

- **Keeping Count**
  This is another way of controlling discussion of routine items in a group that has a history of rambling. Set a limit, i.e., twice, for the number of times an individual may speak on any given question or issue. However, it is important to remember that if someone has very strong feelings on an issue, or special expertise, stifling their expression can be detrimental to the outcome of the decision.

  > **Warning:** *Techniques like the two above should be discussed and supported by the group of participants. Arbitrarily imposing them may seem arrogant and provoke hostility and resistance.*

- **Call to Action**
  When discussion no longer seems productive, any member can call for a vote by making a motion to that effect (see page 155). If the motion isn't seconded, the issue clearly

isn't resolved, but the motion will usually get the discussion back on track. When the discussion bogs down during formation of consensus, state a proposed consensus position and ask for concurrence.

● **Written Input**
This strategy can save time, especially when the input is generated before the meeting. Have each person write brief thoughts on an index card, then collect and review the input.

    Sometimes people fear criticism and retribution that may result if they openly make suggestions opposed by others. These are often the people with the best ideas, and they may be eager to express them anonymously. Written input is ideal for this situation.

● **Delegate**
Not all business requires the involvement of everyone present. Delegate any business that only affects a subgroup. Likewise, don't spend group time on matters that require additional research or specialized expertise. Table these issues until more complete information is available.

Unspoken Messages

Linguistic scholars claim that as much as 90 percent of the meaning of any message is conveyed nonverbally through body language, facial expression, etc. This means that most of the interaction in a meeting is nonverbal, so it is helpful to keep an eye on the group to monitor and clarify responses that may not otherwise be mentioned. This is especially important when controversial issues are being discussed, or when the group is trying to reach consensus.

    If you notice people who haven't said anything for awhile, look withdrawn, or are making faces, check things out. Draw them into the discussion by asking for their thoughts on the current topic. Their silent behavior is affecting the group and is as important as any spoken message. Significant nonverbal reactions to watch for include:

- **Facial Expression**
  Do people look positive, or are they sitting there with frowns? Many don't consider their reservations important enough to discuss, or feel intimidated by factors such as the presence of people outranking them. They may not realize that their thoughts are revealed in their facial expressions.

- **Posture**
  Are people leaning forward in rapt attention, sitting comfortably, or slumping in their chairs? Slumping may indicate fatigue, disgust, or boredom, and it calls for clarification.

- **Body Language**
  Is body language open or closed? Signals such as clenched fists, covered mouth, negative nods, tightly crossed arms, etc., may signal resistance to direction the discussion is taking. Also, watch for signals like a slightly lifted hand, which could mean that the person could use some help breaking into the discussion. Since body language is highly personal, it is often misleading. Be sure to check out the accuracy of your observations.

- **Eye Contact**
  Is the level of eye contact with speakers high or low? Low levels may indicate lack of interest or preoccupation. However, some people, especially men, listen quite well with little eye contact. This is just one of several typical gender differences in meeting behavior and communication style (see page 132).

- **Level of Involvement**
  How actively are individuals and the group as a whole responding? People who seem withdrawn or slow to respond may be resistant, bored, tired, or otherwise out of contact with the process. Asking for their thoughts will either bring them back, or give them the opportunity to clarify their situation and perhaps be excused.

- **Side Conversations**
  Are people talking among themselves during the general discussion? Conversations that don't involve the whole group are distracting, and should not occur. If they do, reconnect the people involved with the group by asking them questions about the discussion topic. Better yet, have a ground rule prohibiting this behavior, and use the ground rule consistently to squelch it immediately (see page 66).

Humor Works

A bit of humor can do wonders to clear the air of tension, build rapport and team spirit, and maintain a generally positive tone. One Meeting Master finds it helpful to appoint a "group jester" ahead of time to be in charge of humor. The role of the jester is to interject humor whenever the group becomes too serious, or when tension builds. This is a challenging role, because the jester must be prepared with jokes or anecdotes for a variety of circumstances. In spite of the intense preparation involved, there are always people eager to volunteer.

Not all humor is constructive. Inappropriate humor is never helpful and can be devastating. It should be avoided, or squelched if it occurs. The following boundaries for humor help keep things light and positive, and may provide useful input for your ground rules:

- **Off-Color Jokes**
  Know your group, but always err on the side of modesty.

Even in single sex groups, many people are offended by off-color jokes and remarks.

- **Ethnic Topics**
  If you have to tell a joke on somebody, make sure that somebody is you.

- **Put-Downs and Sarcasm**
  Zingers (any comment that could provoke the statement, "Just kidding!") may sound funny on the surface, but they hurt and make most people who hear them uncomfortable, even when they aren't personally the target. Be alert to the fact that many zingers are uttered unintentionally, and out of ignorance. If you suspect this is the case, discuss it discretely with the offender to avoid recurrences. If the behavior continues, call for a discussion of the ground rules.

- **Competition**
  This can easily creep in when two or more people begin trying to top each other's stories. Competitive humor is distracting, prolongs meetings, and can lead to harmful competition in other areas (see below).

Process Sabotage

Meetings can be sabotaged at any point from beginning to end. Failure to follow through on commitments can condemn them to failure as surely as lack of planning. In between are a multitude of opportunities for things to bog down, most hinging on the actions and attitudes of the people attending.

Certain common behaviors prolong the meeting, shift the focus away from the stated objectives, or create conflict. Fortunately, there are remedies that can be used to prevent such problems.

Examples of this type of behavior and appropriate remedies are given below:

Behavior	Remedy
"I" Stories When somebody starts telling long war stories, which emphasize heroic actions or flamboyant exploits, the stage is set for one-upmanship. Others are implicitly challenged to match or top them. The resulting frenzy of story-telling sidetracks the process and may provoke a destructive atmosphere of competition.	Refocus on the agenda and ask that business be finished quickly so that socializing can proceed uninterrupted. Refer to the ground rules as needed.
Overstatement Verbose attendees who talk ideas to death alienate others, causing them to tune out or find excuses to leave early.	Review the ground rules at the beginning of meetings and use techniques outlined on pages 87 and 92.
Side Trips and Socializing Highly creative people often have the most trouble sticking to a defined agenda because they are constantly relating what they are hearing to other topics. More often, this behavior signals preoccupation with a personal agenda, lack of personal discipline, or poor meeting management. When social side-issues predominate, the meeting may be filling a primarily social function, and interest in stated issues may be low.	If creativity is generating productive results, let the juices flow, or use bins for holding them (see page 88). For disruptive side-tracks, use the agenda to keep the group on track. When distractions are frequent, or people ignore attempts to get the discussion back on track, the meeting may have ceased to serve a useful purpose. If the meeting does still seem to have value, try redefining the purpose and reviewing the ground rules. If it has outlived its purpose, it may be time to disband (see page 27).

Behavior	Remedy
"They" Statements Hiding behind reports of other people's opinion is a common ploy. It evades personal responsibility for feelings and ideas by creating the illusion of widespread support. This behavior muddies the issues, makes valid decisions virtually impossible, and stirs conflict when opposing sides escalate claims of support.	Clarify the meaning of "they" and negotiate a group agreement on ground rules about personal responsibility for statements (see page 66). When people use these statements, ask them to define which group of people "they" refers to. If they try to speak for the group, with statements like, "We don't want to do such and such," ask them, as diplomatically as possible, when "we" decided that. They'll get the message.
Demeaning Remarks Belittling reactions, interruptions, or abrupt changes of subject that cut somebody off generate a climate of defensive hostility. Killer phrases are especially devastating (see page 105).	Refer to ground rules and refocus on the agenda. If necessary, use conflict resolution techniques or other strategies for reversing negative behavior (see pages 101–103).
Chaos When irrelevant issues are frequently raised, or controversial objections voiced just for the sake of argument, leadership is sabotaged, and it becomes difficult to conduct scheduled business.	See above.

Behavior	Remedy
Indecisive Leadership Some leaders lack the energy, skill, or courage to set an example of focused, assertive, respectful participation by redirecting negative behaviors like those described above. Meetings they lead quickly degenerate into disarray, running overtime, alienating participants, and lacking clear, decisive outcomes.	Back Seat Leadership techniques (see page 128). Leadership training course and/or personal study.

Tips for Unblocking Stuck Meetings

Sometimes meetings run into snags and quit working. The discussion may stray from the designated topic. One or two individuals may begin dominating the discussion. Conflict may flare, ideas may run dry or discussion may hit an impasse. When problems like this arise, these tips will help get the meeting process unblocked and productive again:

- **Use the Ground Rules**
  Refer to the ground rules to tactfully reopen the discussion when anyone begins to dominate (see page 66).

- **Summarize**
  Review previous discussion of the problem or issue under consideration.

- **Restate**
  Use different words to define the objective or desired outcome. This will soothe conflict and channel the discussion in a more productive direction.

- **Review**
  Take another look at all the alternatives and options. See if any new ones come to mind, or whether you may have overlooked any benefits of an existing one.

- **Propose a Solution**
  Suggest a wild idea. Any suggestion, regardless of its relevance, will rekindle people's thinking. If the one you offer doesn't fit, it will give the group a focus for further discussion. A really wild idea may open whole new vistas that would otherwise go unexplored.

- **Brainstorm**
  Generate a whole new list of options to identify previously over looked possibilities (see pages 146–151).

- **Call For Action**
  Call for a vote, suggest a break, request that a volunteer get further information, or have the sponsor of the meeting make a unilateral decision, depending on the situation.

Resolving Conflict

The worst nightmare of meeting leaders is an outbreak of paralyzing controversy that fragments the group and decimates decision-making capability. But the truth is, not all conflict is bad. Well-handled confrontation is actually healthy. Differences of opinion can help the group stay out of ruts or consider all the facts before making decisions.

As a rule of thumb, conflict resolution is found in the job description of the meeting leader or facilitator. Sometimes this person needs help. Fortunately, this function can be filled by anyone with a cool head and the courage to speak up. Whether you are the formal leader or someone doing what has to be done, the guidelines below will help you handle conflict constructively:

- **Don't Hide**
  Bring conflict out into the light. It must be articulated before it can be resolved.

- **Reframe the Situation**
  Help both sides look at things from different perspectives.

- **Stay Calm**
  Hear both sides out without interrupting or commenting. This does not mean allowing them unlimited time to harangue.

- **Restate**
  Check for understanding by repeating both sides of the issue, using your own words. Ask each opposing side to restate the position of the other.

- **Maintain Mutual Respect**
  Don't allow name calling, the use of killer phrases, or other negative, demeaning behavior (see page 105).

- **Empathize**
  Respond to emotional statements made by either side with acceptance and understanding. Conflict is caused as often by personality style differences as anything else. Awareness and acceptance of such differences can help ease the tension.

- **Seek Solutions**
  Ask each side to suggest possible solutions to the dilemma.

- **Use Synergy**
  Seek win/win alternatives to settle the controversy. This means backing up to the basic objectives of each party. Clearly define the needs of each and the priority attached

to each need. Then look for new ways of achieving all of the objectives. This approach differs from compromise. Compromise often generates a sense of winners and losers. Sometimes everyone feels like losers after a compromise. In contrast, everyone leaves a win/win negotiation with a sense of satisfaction, even if the outcome is different from what was originally sought.

Climate Control

Some people seem to arrive at meetings with little thunder clouds over their heads, and their attitude affects the tone of the whole meeting (see page 97). If there is a persistently negative attitude in a group, it is helpful to identify the root cause, especially if it involves the use of killer phrases (see page 105). To find this cause, put the matter of negativity on the agenda and discuss it. Perhaps the negative person(s) feels overlooked or irrelevant, or is irked by factors such as chronically late starting times, arbitrary decisions, or rambling discussions. Or they may disagree with the whole direction things are taking. These feelings are legitimate, and they impact the whole group. Each perception presents a solvable problem, but it is only solvable if it is discussed. In the discussion, focus on *what* is wrong, not *who* is wrong, and avoid any blame or reference to personalities.

For best results in eliminating negative behavior, it should be defined in the group's ground rules (see page 66). Take care to distinguish negative behavior from objective discussion of problems, flawed reasoning, etc. Examples include sexist language, chronic tardiness, or persistent interruptions.

Sometimes simple solutions work. The creative strategies outlined below have been successfully and diplomatically used to neutralize negative attitudes:

- **Persuaders**
  A basket of small, soft sponge balls is placed in the center of the table. Any time someone makes a negative remark (as

defined by the group), group members take balls and throw them at the offender.

This procedure injects humor into the meeting, relieves stress, and lightens the mood. The Meeting Master who shared the technique noted that after only a couple of meetings, the balls remained in the basket, having accomplished the desired results. Months later, they are still kept on the table as a silent reminder.

- **M&M's®**
  The leader brings a bag of M&M's® and places a piece in front of each person attending. As a gesture to human nature, each person is allowed one negative comment during the course of the meeting. After the second such remark, the candy must be eaten. No further negative comments are allowed when your candy is gone. According to a Meeting Master who uses this technique, behavior changes rapidly, because it quickly becomes a status symbol to have a piece of candy at your place when the meeting ends.

- **Umbrella**
  The leader or another person brings an umbrella to the meeting, and when a negative remark is made, opens it, "to keep off the rain." This lightly humorous act isn't needed very often. Unlike the persuader and M&M strategies, this one can be used spontaneously with good effect. If you decide to do this on your own, use it sparingly.

- **Tension Breaks**
  Both planned and unplanned tension breaks are used very successfully by a Meeting Master who often conducts planning meetings that run anywhere from four hours to several days. Planned breaks are held on schedule. Unplanned ones are called when people get restless, edgy, or the process bogs down in some other way. In either case, "games" or exercise activities are planned for 10 to 15 minutes. A collection of "toys," consisting of such items as sponge footballs, bubble blowers, slinkies, etc., is kept by the group for these occasions.

This same group has made a ground rule giving members permission to engage in activities such as doodling, modeling with PlayDoh® (which is kept on hand for the purpose), etc., to release their creative juices and relieve tension during prolonged task-oriented or planning meetings. The ground rule is vital to keep these behaviors from creating a distraction.

These techniques barely scratch the surface of possibilities. They get rapid results when used as described. Use them when the negativity is a personality trait rather than a reaction to a specific situation. You can also use them as a starting point to brainstorm your own solution. Just make sure your chosen solution doesn't belittle or seriously embarrass anyone. If the problem keeps cropping up, take a closer look at root causes. These may include underlying conflict or competition between individuals, or the inclusion of some person whose talents would be better used other ways.

Helpful Hint

If only one person in a group is persistently negative, the issue should be discussed with the person privately before bringing it up in the group. It may stem from personal problems or some other factor that would be embarrassing or otherwise inappropriate to discuss in a group.

If and when the issue is raised with the group, alert the target person ahead of time!

Killer Phrases

Certain kinds of phrases are sudden death to a trusting climate or spontaneous and honest expression of ideas. These killer phrases quickly dampen creativity. Your ground rules should prohibit their use. When there are no ground rules, expose killer phrases immediately for what they are with a response such as, "Wow, that sure sounds like a killer phrase!"

Your willingness to keep things out in the open will encourage others to be open.

Killer phrases can be distinguished from positive disagreement or a statement of realistic limitations by their demeaning or condescending tone. They usually indicate an unwillingness to consider new ideas.

Examples of typical killer phrases follow:

- "That's a really dumb idea!"

- "That couldn't possibly work!"

- "Nobody in their right mind would try that."

- "We just don't do things that way here."

- "Who have you been talking to? Some New Age Meditation Guru?"

- "What do you mean? You don't like the way I do things?"

- "Jack would never approve of an idea like that."

- "Well, it doesn't matter, because they'll never let us do it anyway."

- "No, I have a much better idea..."

Strategies for Effective Delegation

The same delegation tactics that get good results for managers will work well for meeting leaders. When a project team, or similar group, is formed of people who report to different supervisors, accountability for assignments is an important issue. To avoid confusion, it should be clearly stated in the team ground rules that members will follow-through on commitments accepted within the team meetings. If necessary, the supervisors involved should also agree to these ground rules.

There may be times when you chair a group consisting of members outside your personal sphere of control and lack ground rules to back you up. In this situation, the following guidelines will serve as an interim solution until you can negotiate ground rules. They will help you make effective assignments and increase the likelihood of timely and satisfactory compliance:

- **Be Specific**
  Clearly identify the responsibility involved.

- **Stand Firm**
  Don't play martyr by bailing people out and letting them dump responsibility back in your lap. Encourage them to find a way to fulfill their obligation.

- **Seek Volunteers**
  Involve the group in the delegation process, explaining choices and/or asking for volunteers. An Action Items Bin is ideal for bringing order to the process of soliciting volunteers (see page 88). Sometimes, when a big project is at hand, it is a good idea to prime the pump by soliciting a few volunteers before the meeting.

- **Distribute the Load**
  Giving all the assignments to the same trusty, dependable few leads to burn-out. It also invites overload, which will make it impossible for them to meet all their deadlines and quality requirements. One way to avoid this dilemma is to use the Action Items bin.

- **Look for Shirkers**
  Be alert to people who tend to hide when there is work to be done. Check out their situation. They may be legitimately busy, they may not be reliable, or they may just need a little coaxing to do a terrific job.

- **Deal with Dissent**
  Allow complainers the opportunity to do something active about their dissatisfaction rather than passively sitting on the sidelines and complaining.

- **Stay Out of the Way**
  Delegate as much authority as possible, and then don't breathe down the neck of the person doing the job. Remaining involved with every detail, or calling for constant reports from a person of proven competence is demeaning and demoralizing. It also creates bottlenecks.

- **Express Appreciation**
  Give abundant credit and recognition to those who deserve it.

Follow-up for Meetings

Unless follow-up action is taken on decisions and plans, meetings are a waste of time and money. To ensure that your meetings produce the results you need, use these follow-up strategies:

- **Schedule Follow-up**
  Include reports about follow-up actions on future meeting agendas. Schedule times for any necessary phone calls and letters to ensure follow-up action is being taken.

- **Be Clear**
  Make assignments specific, with clear deadlines.

- **Confirm Assignments**
  Send memos promptly after the meeting that reconfirm assignments. If people know you routinely do this for everyone, nobody will feel paranoid or insulted.

- **Confirm Agreement**
  If you don't receive confirmation of the message within a few days, phone or talk in person.

- **Confirm Concurrence**
  When you delegate assignments to people within your organization, but outside your reporting chain, consider sending memos to their supervisors. This creates visibility for you, and may help the person involved clear the time to complete the task. However, memos to supervisors also carry some political risk if they are awkwardly handled. To avoid either the appearance of grandstanding or implying weakness in the people involved, get their concurrence before sending these executive memos.

- **Use Discretion**
  When you are unsure of a person's reliability, delegate low risk assignments to check it out.

- **Motivate Acceptance**
  Avoid imposing arbitrary assignments. It's more effective to stimulate enthusiasm for the idea so the person readily accepts the responsibility.

- **Keep Records**
  Both personal notes and official minutes come in handy when there is any confusion about who is supposed to do what by when.

Meeting Wrap-up

Ending a meeting without a wrap-up sequence is like walking away from a sales call without asking the prospect to buy anything. In both cases, people are left hanging and time is wasted. To ensure that decisions made at meetings serve their full useful purpose, conclude the meeting with these simple steps:

- **Review the Agenda**
  Run down the agenda to make sure all the items were covered and review any decisions and plans that were made.

- **Review Follow-up Plans**
  Double check to see that all the bases are covered, and that everyone agrees on the steps to be taken.

- **Reconfirm Responsibilities**
  Clarify understanding of follow-up actions to be taken by individuals, including deadlines and any reporting dates for interim steps.

- **Ask for Input**
  Conduct an evaluation of the meeting in general, asking for thoughts on ways to continuously improve the process.

- **Set the Next Agenda**
  Ending a meeting by discussing the agenda for the following one simplifies the leader's job. Using the Agenda Bin format virtually automates this process (see page 88).

- **Empty the Action Items Bin**
  Review all items in the Action Items Bin and assign them appropriately.

- **Empty Other Bins**
  Depending on the time available, you can either deal with everything in every bin, or make group decisions to postpone some or all of the items.

Evaluating the Meeting

Use the following sample evaluation checklist as it is, or adapt it to identify ways your meetings can be made more efficient and productive. Continuing groups will find it helpful to schedule the checklist as a regular agenda item. The scores lend themselves well to quality analysis tools, like Pareto or control charts.

One Meeting Master uses a similar form at the end of his meetings. He goes around the room and asks for scores, then asks those with the highest and lowest scores to explain their scores. He makes a bar graph as the results are being gathered. Graphs are kept in a file and periodically reviewed to spot patterns that indicate areas the group needs to concentrate on improving.

When you attend a meeting where you aren't in a position to hold a formal evaluation, you can still use the form as a personal learning tool. Critique the meeting yourself to see how you would do it better another time. Though some groups and/or leaders may resist the idea of formal evaluation, you may be able to suggest one small change at a time. Eventually you will accomplish great things.

Meeting Evaluation Form

Instructions: Rate each item below on a scale of 1-5, with 1 signifying a large need for improvement; 3 signifying adequate performance; and 5 signifying optimum performance. Add the individual ratings for an overall score, and target low-scoring items for specific improvement efforts.

_____ Did the meeting have a focused purpose?
_____ Was the purpose clear to you?
_____ Was the stated purpose achieved?
_____ What was the quality of the decisions we made?
_____ Did it have a planned agenda?
_____ Did we stick to the schedule?
_____ Did the discussion stay on track?
_____ Did participants keep their input concise and to the point?
_____ Did everyone participate?
_____ Were disagreements or conflicts smoothly resolved?
_____ Were responsibilities shared?
_____ Did it make good use of attendees' abilities?
_____ Was provision made for following-up and ensuring
         accountability?
_____ Was the meeting fun?
_____ TOTAL

Remarks:

5

Personally Speaking

Two people were overheard talking as they walked down the hall after a task force meeting. "You know," said the first, "we've been having these meetings at least once a week for more than a year, and I think today was the first time we've ever really accomplished anything!"

"Yes," agreed the second, "Marion hit the nail on the head by sending that agenda out early and insisting we each do our part to get ready. I'll have to admit that I hadn't been doing much more than show up. But it really didn't take any longer to get that report together ahead of time than it would have later, and it sure smoothed things out."

"Did you notice how much less talking people did? I guess we've just been thinking out loud, spending each meeting planning the next. Maybe that's not such a great idea. The way things went today, we may actually get the job done and quit having to meet."

"What? And miss all that fun?...I can hardly wait!"

Did you ever stop to think about the power of the people sitting in a meeting? The most talented leader may plan to perfection and facilitate with finesse, but if the people involved in the meeting aren't prepared and cooperative, the process is doomed to failure or mediocrity.

Principle #4:
Take personal responsibility for meeting outcomes.

The leader will obviously appreciate the effort you put into preparing for the meeting, but the most compelling reasons for

113

getting your ducks in order are far more personal. It's a rare day when you attend a meeting without some personal objective you want to achieve. You may want to lobby for some cause, propose a new project, support another person, or impress someone with your brilliance. You may need information or want to make sure you don't get extra work dumped on you in your absence. Whatever you want to achieve, you'll do it better if you have laid the groundwork before the meeting.

You will also do it better if your communication skills are sharp and if you know how to get a meeting back on track when the leader falls down on the job. This section has guidelines for personal preparation, effective communication, persuasion tactics, staying in control of a presentation, and Back Seat Leadership.

Personal Preparation

Your advance preparation shortens the meeting and saves time for everyone. It also makes you look good. Groups with ground rules should have one stating that every member is responsible for personal preparation.

But lots of meetings don't have ground rules, especially if they are one-of-a-kind. Personal preparation is just as important for these meetings. Begin your personal preparation by reviewing the agenda well ahead of time. If you haven't received one, call the meeting leader and ask for it! As you review the agenda, consider the relevance of each item to be sure the meeting is worth attending (see page 28). When you do decide to attend, answer these questions for each relevant item:

● **What is my position?**
  Clarify your position on the item, stating it concisely and clearly.

- **What support do I have?**
  Identify sources of support for your position. This support may consist of written material and documentation or verbal support during the meeting. If you are counting on verbal support, check before the meeting to make sure it is predictable and reliable. It may also be advantageous to confer with those who will oppose your plan. Understanding their objections allows you to respond more constructively, and you may even resolve your differences.

- **What are the benefits?**
  List the benefits of your position for all concerned.

- **What objections are likely?**
  Prepare to address any opposing points of view you can anticipate.

- **How else can this objective be met?**
  Draft at least one alternative position or "Plan B."

- **How should I present my views?**
  Prepare to present and discuss your views within the stated time limitations.

Where to Sit

People choose seats at meetings for all sorts of reasons. Some want to sit next to a particular person; others sit wherever there is an empty seat. Some prefer a certain chair; others choose a seat to be far away from someone they want to avoid, or to be close to the coffee pot. Some select seats to increase their success in achieving their objectives. These suggestions will help you choose a seat to accomplish your specific purpose:

- **Exert Influence**
  Sit directly across the table from someone you want to influence. This gives the maximum opportunity for eye contact, an important influence factor. If that seat is taken, the person is sitting at the end of a very long table, or the seats are in rows, a good second choice is on the right of the person (left for a southpaw).

- **Get Attention**
  Sit directly across from, or directly next to, someone you want to have notice you.

- **Build Trust**
  Some people recommend sitting to the right of a person when you want to generate a feeling of trust. This recommendation dates back to medieval times when people of questionable loyalty were seated on the left because right-handed people would normally thrust a dagger to the left. Thus the origin of the term "Right Hand Man."

- **Identify Yourself with Leadership**
  Sitting next to the leader, especially to the right of the leader, puts you in view as people look at the leader, generating subliminal connection.

- **Networking**
  This practical objective is best achieved by sitting next to anyone with whom you want to strengthen a relationship.

- **Exert Back Seat Leadership**
  Sitting directly opposite the leader puts you in a strong position to intervene and counter the lack of strong leadership.

- **Miscellaneous**
  When you don't have a compelling reason for choosing one seat over another, sit wherever you are comfortable.

Masterful Participation

Meeting participants bear as much responsibility for making meetings succeed as the leader does. Use the following tips to make your contributions further both your own purposes and those of the group:

● **Be Prepared**

   – Seek out as much information as you can before the meeting so you can discuss the issues knowledgeably and productively.

   – When you present proposals or reports, prepare handouts and visual aids to support and clarify your point.

● **Plan Ahead**
   Give the leader a list of topics you want to discuss far enough ahead for them to be included on the agenda.

● **Be on Time**
   If you will be attending the whole meeting, arrive a few minutes early.

● **Be Honest**
   Express your views and feelings openly, honestly, and concisely. Honesty goes hand-in-glove with diplomacy.

● **Don't Dominate**
   Take personal responsibility for keeping your input terse. If you have trouble expressing yourself clearly and concisely, participating in a Toastmaster club will be enormously helpful (see page 213).

● **Be Positive**
   Present your ideas optimistically. Don't dwell on past failures or tear down other people's ideas.

- **Use Synergy**
  Build on the ideas of others. When you have an idea relating to a topic other than the one under discussion, or to a person or project outside the meeting, write it down and put it in the Synergism Bin (see page 89).

- **Express Appreciation**
  Let others know when you are impressed with something they say or do, or when they have been helpful to you.

- **Watch Body Language**
  Be alert to nonverbal signals of others, and help the leader encourage input from quiet members of the group (see page 94).

- **Stay Flexible**
  Keep an open mind, propose and explore alternate options, and move from preconceived ideas to synergistic win/win solutions.

How to Avoid Being Interrupted

If someone tries to interrupt you while you are speaking during a meeting, assertive behavior is called for. That is assuming you have been sticking to the point and not belaboring the issue. Tolerating occasional interruptions may be expedient. When you continually allow yourself to be cut off without protest, both your own effectiveness and the group process are weakened.

To hold your ground, reach out with your palm raised and fingers spread, and say something like the statements below:

- "Hold that thought!"

- "Just a second."

- "Please let me finish."

If the person starts talking louder in an attempt to drown you out, increase your own volume. Don't let the situation escalate into a shouting match. Before it gets to the point of yelling, stop talking and stare at the interrupter. This will almost always put a stop to the behavior.

This assertive behavior may be stressful for people who are not used to using it, but with practice it can become quite natural. Many people find it helpful to visualize the process in advance, or even practice the sequence with a supportive partner.

Interruptions are always detrimental to the group process, and should be prohibited in the ground rules (see page 66). The meeting leader or facilitator should always invoke the ground rules to stop such behavior, but if they don't, do it yourself. If interruptions and harassing questions persist, use negotiation skills to resolve the differences. Make it clear what you are doing by using clarifying statements like, "Let me see if I understand. Jess, you are saying... and Pat, you are saying...."

Improve Your Listening Skills

The whole point of communication is to generate shared understanding. While stating yourself clearly obviously helps generate shared understanding, by itself it's not enough. To understand others as they intend, and vice versa, you must *listen*, carefully and skillfully.

Listening is the most often used communication skill, and the least taught. In an average day, people in business spend several hours listening. Failure to listen well is the most common cause of costly mistakes, missed deadlines, and irritation. Poor listening is especially prevalent and detrimental during meetings because at any given time, only one person can talk and many must listen.

Here are some tips for improving your listening, and ensuring shared understanding, in or out of meetings:

● **Listen More than You Speak**
   Be sparing with your own words.

- **Focus on the Speaker**
  Set aside your own worries and internal distractions.

- **Don't Interrupt**
  Be patient, and use nonverbal signals if you want to add
  a thought.

- **Show Interest**
  Use facial expression, posture, nods, and interjections such as
  "uh-huh," or "hmmm," to let the speaker know you are
  listening and interested.

- **Eye Contact**
  Maintaining a high level of eye contact lets the speaker know
  you are listening, and helps keep your attention focused.

- **Consider the Speaker's Point of View**
  When you disagree with the speaker, or have differences of
  background and experience, it is especially important to try
  to understand the other person's perspective.

- **Read Between the Lines**
  Notice body language and other nonverbal cues of underlying
  messages (see page 94).

- **Be Empathetic**
  Respond to emotional statements and nonverbal messages with
  statements showing that you understand and accept the feelings
  being expressed.

- **Avoid Assumptions**
  Stereotyping, jumping to conclusions, and other mental
  shortcuts can prevent shared understanding.

- **Clarify Mixed Messages**
  When nonverbal signals don't match the spoken message,
  ask questions to determine the source of the confusion.

- **Use Reality Checks**
  Ask questions or restate the message to make sure you share understanding with the speaker.

- **Be Honest**
  When you are short on time, or really don't feel like listening, say so. Make arrangements to listen later, then be sure to keep your word.

Questions Forms

Learning to ask questions well is one of the most useful communication skills a person can acquire. Questions serve a multitude of purposes. They are useful for obtaining information, checking understanding, and generally finding out what other people think. Furthermore, as successful sales people know, they could be the most powerful persuasion tool in existence. People are more strongly convinced when they are led to develop a conclusion for themselves.

Questions work equally well with a single other person or in groups of people at meetings. The following table gives examples of several types of questions you will find useful in different types of situations:

Sample Question Formats

Type	Goal	Format
Factual	To get information.	Begins with "what, where, when, why, who, how and how much."
Explor- atory	To get additional information or to broaden discussion.	"How would that help?" "How would you go about doing that?" "What other things should be considered?"

Type	Goal	Format
Justi-fication	To get proof, to challenge old ideas and to generate new ones.	"What makes you say that?" "Where did you hear that?" "Have you actually tried it?"
Leading	To introduce a thought of your own.	"Would this be a possible solution?" "Have you tried this?"
Hypothe-tical	To test assumptions or suppositions.	"What would happen if we did it this way?" "If I do it this other way, will it still work?"
Alternative	To reach a decision or agreement.	"Which of these plans do you think is best?" "Would you rather get together on Monday or Wednesday?"
Consensual	To develop common agreement. To take action.	"Do we all agree that this is what we want to do?" "Is there anything preventing us from getting started now?"

Get Your Views Accepted

There isn't much point in attending meetings if you don't care about the outcome of at least some of the issues. So, whether you are meeting with one person or one hundred, it is vital to know how to get your views accepted.

The tips below will help you sharpen your skills and reinforce your intuitive approach. Use the ones most appropriate for each situation:

● **Keep it Simple**
State your case directly and specifically.

● **Ask Questions**
Use questions to find out how people think and feel before you try to convince them of anything.

● **Appeal to Emotions**
People often base decisions on feelings more than facts.

● **Use Logic**
Support emotional appeals with logic.

● **Diversify Your Approach**
Visual aids and visual imagery in your speech support your case and increase retention. Demonstrations and other sensory input also strengthen your message.

● **Be Cautious About Statistics**
Use statistical data sparingly and only to support examples and case histories. Keep it simple unless your presentation requires a high degree of technical information.

● **Consider Their Bias**
Present only one side of an argument when:

– You are viewed as an authority on the subject.

– Your audience initially agrees with you and will not be exposed to the other side.

Present both sides of the issue when the audience:

- Is opposed to the idea.

- Is well informed about the topic.

- Is likely to hear the other side.

● **Experiment**
Propose a small-scale test of your idea to demonstrate its effectiveness.

● **Meet on Neutral Ground**
When seeking a favor or approval for an idea, hold meetings on neutral ground such as a conference room or restaurant to keep things on an equal footing (see page 35).

● **Spell it Out**
Draw conclusions for your audience, unless you know they are well informed on the topic. Use a lot of questions to do this.

● **Close the Sale**
Ask for action at the end of your request. Don't assume people will comply without being directly asked.

Visual Aids

Visual aids are invaluable when you are making a point or presenting a proposal, because people think in pictures as well as words. Research has shown that retention increases several fold when visual aids are used, so anything you can do to provide visual input will increase your effectiveness by keeping their attention better, and increasing their understanding of your message.

Several forms of visual aids are summarized below with hints on using each well:

● **Gestures and Verbal Imagery**
Don't underestimate the importance of these simple techniques, which are always available and appropriate. They are effective alone, and enhance any of the techniques below.

● **Handouts**
Technical information, such as spreadsheets, charts, letters, and reports, is most effective when presented as handouts. Unless the surprise element is important, distribute complex material ahead of time, so people can read it and prepare questions. When you have supplementary handouts intended for later use, distribute them at the end of the meeting to keep them from becoming distractions.

● **Chalk or Marker Board**
Spontaneous illustrations and simple information lend themselves well to this medium. Make sure everyone can see what you write or draw, and use fresh markers that don't squeak.

● **Flip Chart**
This versatile tool is useful with small to medium-sized groups. Flip charts are good for brainstorming, recording lists of input during workshops, and illustrating points. They are especially effective when sheets are prepared ahead of time with cartoons, diagrams, or artistically lettered bullet lists. Check for fresh markers, and use the following tips:

– Paper with a pale blue grid helps keep lines straight and aids in layout. These pads are available in most office supply stores for the same price as plain ones.

– Keep format simple, with large writing.

- Leave at least two blank pages between those prepared ahead to prevent show-through and make space available for spontaneous notes.

- Use Post-It™ notes or paper clips to mark prepared pages for easy access.

- Dark colors are more easily seen.

- Presentation notes can be lightly penciled on flip chart pages ahead of time. If you will be making your presentation in a dimly lit room, make sure they are dark enough to be seen.

- Use masking tape to post torn-off sheets on the wall for brainstorming sessions, or use vinyl sheets, which adhere to literally any surface by static electricity. If you use dry-erase markers, vinyl sheets can be wiped clean and reused.

● **Overhead Slides**
Overhead slides don't require a darkened room, and with an appropriately large screen, the image can be seen by an audience of any size. For crisply professional illustrations, prepare overhead slides on a computer and laser print them. Color printing technology is rapidly improving and decreasing in cost, so for important presentations, consider this option. These tips will help you display any overhead slides more effectively:

- Make sure neither you nor the projector is blocking the view.

- Keep slides simple, using short bullet-lists, graphs, or pictures. Avoid lengthy paragraphs of typewritten material or complex diagrams with tiny type.

- Print borders around edges and use a type size large enough to fill most of the slide. Colored films, cardboard frames, and color printing add extra punch.

- Always face the audience, not the screen.

- When several minutes will pass between slides, turn off the projector.

- Use a telescoping pointer or place a pointer directly on the slide. Don't point with your finger or hand.

- Use a sheet of cardboard to progressively uncover points on bullet lists.

- Presentation notes can be written on cardboard frames.

- Have a spare bulb available.

- **35mm Slides**
  This medium gives the highest quality image, but requires a darkened room. This is the best way to show photographs, although color copier technology is rapidly closing the gap with the ability to make high-resolution overhead slides of photographs. Keep other material simple, as above.

- **Computer-Driven LCD Projection Panels**
  This cutting edge technology is becoming widely accessible. Software packages are available to create computerized slides (use guidelines for overhead slides) and manage their presentation. Other media, such as video, can be displayed with the projection panel. Some panels can be used for rear projection to reduce visual clutter in front of the screen. This requires a very deep room. The panels work best with an ultra-bright projector.

- **Videotapes**
  Commercially available or custom-made videotapes are useful for demonstrations, training, previews, and assorted other applications. To make sure everyone in a larger group can see adequately, use large screen projection or multiple monitors. Tell people how long the video will run before it begins.

- **Demonstration Models**
  When people actually see an object or process, it is easier to understand and much more memorable.

  – Make sure models can be seen.

  – Passing models around may distract the group. It is usually more effective to carry them around and then place them on a table where they can be easily seen.

Back Seat Leadership

In a perfect world everyone would take turns in perfect order, speaking concisely and clearly at all times. Leaders would be unnecessary. But right now, since we don't live in this perfect world, leaders are still necessary.

Unfortunately, even leaders aren't perfect. When you attend a meeting and the leader drops the ball, your assistance as a Back Seat Leader may be critical. The following tips illustrate tactful ways of exercising this option.

Before the meeting:

- **Obtain the Agenda**
  Contact the leader and request a copy of the agenda if it isn't forthcoming in a timely fashion. Offer to assist in drafting one if it hasn't been done.

During the meeting:

● **Guide the Discussion**
Clarify statements of other participants, reflecting and relating them back to the agenda (see page 85).

● **Set a Good Example**
Express your own ideas concisely and clearly, keeping them to the point.

● **Keep Notes**
Your own record is especially important and helpful when no minutes are taken. These notes enable you to track action and keep an eye on things, whether the leader does or not (see page 79).

● **Show Respect**
Avoid direct confrontation over leadership issues in front of the group. If the subject arises, give the leader a way to save face. If it must be discussed, it is best done in private.

● **Review Progress**
If the leader hasn't already done so, clarify the points covered during the meeting by summarizing them at the end.

After the meeting:

● **Follow-Up**
Contact and coordinate efforts with people whose responsibilities for follow-up action have direct relevance to you. Sometimes you may have a vested interest in the outcome of someone else's assignment, and may not be sure that it will be completed. In this case, tactfully arrange conversations with the relevant people and discuss their progress in meeting the objectives. Knowing of your interest and observation may be the extra nudge they need to come through with results.

6

Meeting Tune-Up Tool Kit

There is no such a thing as an ordinary meeting. In the first place, the purpose and objectives of any given meeting will differentiate it from other meetings, and may call for some special procedural adaptation. Furthermore, even a routine business meeting has something besides the changing agenda items that is unique about it. Some meetings brim with enthusiasm. Creative ideas flow with the gusto of a stream during spring melt. Other times, conflict erupts, and tempers flare. Now and then, even when everyone has done their homework and come prepared, the whole process hits a snag and virtually grinds to a halt. Obviously, such a diversity of challenges calls for a variety of meeting management tools beyond such basics as preparing an agenda, sticking to it, or enforcing time limits.

Principle #5:
If your meeting isn't working, try another tool.

This section will give you an assortment of tools with special applications for various meeting situations. When you have these tactics available, you can recognize special needs and meet them in the most efficient, effective way. You will find tips on handling specific kinds of meetings, such as brainstorming and business meetings. Also included are guidelines for forming consensus, and follow-up for ensuring the long-term success of your meetings.

There are even helpful hints for applying Total Quality Management (TQM) principles to meetings. These principles will improve your meetings, whether or not you have implemented any form of TQM in your organization.

131

You won't need each of these tools for every meeting, but knowing where to find them when the need arises will do more than help you cope – it will identify you as a true Meeting Master.

Genderspeak

Social scientists have documented gender-related differences in meeting participation styles, which may affect the outcomes of meetings you attend. These differences are primarily concerned with the use of language. Men and women appear to speak the same language, in this case English. However, there are many ways they differ in their use and understanding of it. Although it is dangerous to stereotype behavior, and communication style varies widely from one person to another, some general observations are valid. Understanding a few of these differences can help you make sense of some baffling situations.

Awareness of these differences can be especially useful when you attend meetings that include both men and women. It can help you get your points across more effectively and more clearly understand the thinking and behavior of other attendees. It may also give some women courage to participate more assertively in meetings, while reminding some men to be more alert for signs that others have something to say.

Typical differences are listed in the following table, along with helpful hints:

Difference	Helpful Hints
Taking Turns Women generally wait for a sign of recognition by the previous speaker before beginning to talk. Men have less hesitation. They are more inclined to either interrupt, or jump in at the slightest hint of a pause.	When you are leading a mixed meeting, be especially alert for quiet women. Due to the "difficulty" of breaking into the discussion in male-dominated groups, some women tend not to participate unless they are specifically asked for their opinion.

Difference	Helpful Hints
Balance Research has consistently shown that men in groups speak more than twice as often as women. Their shortest turns tend to be longer than the women's longest.	Address the general issue of equity in length of turns in the ground rules.
Content Groups composed primarily of women tend to spend relatively more time discussing process and relationship issues than male-dominated groups, which tend to focus more narrowly on task-related topics.	When you have a mixed meeting group, women may be able to make a significant contribution in calling attention to group process and help avoid some needless confrontations about task-related matters. Some male Meeting Masters find it advantageous to team up with a female "process monitor" when they are leading meetings (see page 41).
Reaction to Problems When men hear about a problem, they want to offer advice and "fix it." The typical feminine style is to empathize and tell stories of similar events.	Use a structured problem-solving process to avoid overindulgence in empathy and/or "quick-fixes" that may not adequately address the problem (see pages 135, 141).
Information Sharing Women are more likely to freely share and even volunteer information that they think will be helpful to others. Many men exercise personal power by controlling information and playing their cards much closer to their chests. Thus "helpful" women may seem gossipy, loose-tongued, or domineering to many men. Conversely, many women feel paranoid when men seem to hoard information.	Formulating the agenda and conferring with people ahead of time about how they should prepare will optimize the amount of information that is shared. So will a healthy, trusting climate.

Rut Busters

When routine meetings are unfocused, prolonged, and generally tedious, it's time for a culture change. Sometimes just seeing the need for change, and taking a step like discussing some new ground rules with the group, will do the trick. But most of the time, instigating change seems about as easy as swimming the English Channel. Even when people are convinced of the need, a lot of calls for change provoke cries like, "We've always done it this way!" Fortunately, this resistance can usually be overcome with tact, persuasion, and empathy (see page 27).

     Whether you lead meetings, or simply attend them, the following problem-solving guidelines give you positive steps for facilitating change and streamlining your meeting routine:

- **Explain the Need**
  State the case for implementing change, and focus on the disadvantages of the status quo.

- **Define the Problem**
  The first step in solving any problem is defining it accurately. This can be especially challenging when several people are involved, because each person may view the problem differently. But if they can't agree on the definition of the problem, they are unlikely to agree on a solution.

- **Define the Cause**
  Conduct a discussion to explore the specific root cause(s) of the problem.

- **Define the Objective**
  When routine meetings slip into a rut, it is often because the original purpose for having the meetings has changed or become obsolete. Taking a fresh look at the purpose and

objectives can get things back on track (see page 20). It's also possible that reexamining the purpose will show that the meetings have outlived their usefulness and should be abandoned. If you do decide to continue meeting, draft a mission statement (or update an existing one) to clarify the reason for the group to continue meeting.

● **Define the Desired Outcome**
Formulate a vision statement of what the group collectively would like to see itself become. The process of forming consensus to define a shared vision is highly energizing. Motivation and cohesiveness generally increase as members strive together to attain newly defined goals.

● **Formulate Strategy**
Use brainstorming and problem-solving techniques to define alternative strategies for bringing about the change (see page 146).

● **Implement the Plan**
Select one or more strategies and begin implementation. If there are too many to tackle all at once, start with the one that will have the greatest pay-off.

● **Form Consensus**
Decisions about guidelines and strategies for the future of the group are the sort of agreements that are best reached by consensus (see page 142).

The strength of this approach is the personal investment that results when attendees participate in formulating a direction and approach. This increases acceptance and enthusiastic support of the new direction, enhancing success.

Dealing with Indecisiveness

Difficulty in making decisions is a common affliction. Sometimes there is just one decision that is especially hard to make. Other times, groups fall into a syndrome of chronically delaying decisions, putting them off until a later meeting, or not making them at all. Many factors can contribute to this situation, including discussions that ramble, hidden agendas, lack of important information, or fear of change and unknowable outcomes, to name a few.

The solution for this sort of impasse depends largely on its cause. Guidelines for conflict resolution (see page 101), problem-solving (see pages 134, 141), or consensus generation (see page 142), may be helpful in addition to the following general guidelines:

- **Distribute the Agenda Early**
  When one or more individuals consistently delay decisions to confer with superiors, this strategy is especially important. Many times they will be able to get input on acceptable options before the meeting, and arrive empowered to make a decision with no further delay.

- **Involve Decision-Makers**
  Whenever possible, involve the actual decision-makers in the meeting. This speeds up the process, and avoids the danger that information will be distorted as it works its way through several repetitions.

- **Confer Ahead**
  Preliminary discussion is particularly helpful in situations like the previous one. A short conference provides the opportunity to answer as many questions as possible in advance and find out what further information the decision makers will need.

- **Segment Decisions**
  When decisions are large and complex, they can be overwhelming. Break them down into component parts.

This builds momentum on simple things and gets the process flowing again. A facilitated process such as the Analytic Heirarchy Process can help resolve complicated decisions (see page 213).

● **Look at Organizational Culture**
Individuals and organizations that are heavily into micro-management often have morale problems, as well as bogged down decision-making processes. Organizations that practice empowerment as part of their culture have fewer problems with group indecision and its related delays. On an organizational level, empowerment is a concept that must be understood and practiced at the executive level before it can become a pervasive way of doing business.

Facts About Facilitation

Facilitation is a special form of leadership that requires a combination of technical skill, objectivity and, sometimes, guts. It involves managing the discussion process from definition of a problem, through identification and evaluation of alternatives, to a final decision. Although this process is not inherently difficult, maintaining the appropriate level of objectivity can be.

When the designated leader of a group has a high investment in the outcome, it may be impossible to maintain the level of objectivity necessary for serving as facilitator. Likewise, political considerations and reporting relationships may constrain the discussion. When representatives from multiple levels and/or different departments of the organization are involved, calling in an outside facilitator is recommended. For ordinary purposes, a facilitator from another area of your organization can fill the role, if a sufficiently skilled person is available. Check with the human resources department to find an internal facilitator.

There are two situations where it is virtually mandatory to call in an external facilitator who has no ties to your organization.

The first concerns meetings that involve executive level management meetings with people from lower levels of the organization to make decisions with vital strategic significance. Few people are willing to argue with the C.E.O.! The second is when complicated problem-solving or planning requires specialized expertise and techniques that are only available through an external source.

Unfortunately, at this time, the only reliable way of finding a competent external facilitator is to network with colleagues in other companies or professional organizations. Many consultants offer facilitation services as part of a comprehensive package. However, consultants working with your organization on other projects are not generally ideal candidates. If the meeting has any connection with a project they are consulting on, they have a vested interest in the outcome. They may be as biased as anyone inside the organization. Although there are consultants who are able to separate their thinking enough to remain fully objective as a facilitator, this may not be the best use of their expertise. It is often worth the extra expense to use an independent third party as your facilitator, and to include your consultant as a resource person in the meeting. Regardless of who you use as a facilitator, remember that the facilitation process should never be used as a platform for promoting further services.

There are a number of ways of becoming skilled at facilitation. Many fine training programs exist, ranging in length from a day to a week. But, it takes more than just a workshop to make a good facilitator. Some of the best facilitators have an intuitive knack for the process. They have developed their skills through a combination of trial-and-error, picking up pointers from others, and taking advantage of every opportunity to practice.

The following list of attributes of a good facilitator can help you make a good selection for your group:

- **Objective**
  A competent facilitator is able to set personal biases aside and operate strictly within the bounds of group-generated ideas.

- **Technically Skilled**
  Facilitators should be trained in techniques such as advanced brainstorming, force-field analysis, or conflict resolution strategies. Ideally, to back-up personal skills and lend structure to the discussion and decision process, the facilitator should have some system, such as the Analytic Hierarchy Process (AHP) available (see page 213).

- **Gutsy**
  Strong facilitators are not intimidated by authority figures, domineering individuals, or other challenging participants. Facilitators must be willing and able to tell anyone in the room, from the C.E.O. to hourly workers, to sit back and wait for a turn, listen more carefully, or otherwise alter their behavior.

- **Observant**
  The facilitator must be attuned to individuals who are hesitant to openly express ideas, less articulate than others, or otherwise reluctant to participate. These reluctant participants must be brought into the process if it is to be completely successful.

Total Quality Meeting Management

Using a Total Quality paradigm, the meeting is viewed as a process, as illustrated in Figure 1. At one end is a series of needs, questions, and resource information. In the planning stage, information is sorted and decisions about procedure are made. During the meeting, this information is discussed and considered in relation to the needs and questions. The end result is decisions that answer the questions and define strategies for meeting the needs. If meetings aren't producing satisfactory results, the cause(s) may lie anywhere along this process line, from the quality of the raw information, questions, or planning, to skill levels in decision-making or implementation.

The only way to improve results is to improve the process at points where it is bogged down. Help for doing this is found throughout the Handbook. Chapters One, Two and parts of Four cover planning and preparation. Improvement of the meeting conduct phase is covered in Chapter Three and parts of Four.

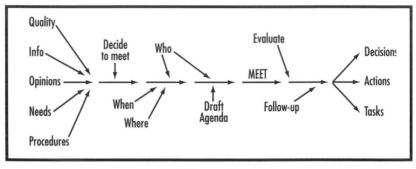

Figure 1

    Applying Total Quality concepts to meetings takes the element of accountability further than usual. This is done by identifying measurable criteria to define each element of the meeting process, i.e., whether the agenda is formulated and distributed, or time limits for participants. Other criteria may address outcomes, i.e., concluding the scheduled business within the designated time, and without the need for unanticipated follow-up meetings.

    As the process unfolds, each element is evaluated for conformance to the relevant criteria. Any time it doesn't conform, a defective outcome has occurred. For example, consider the following criterion for preparation: "Participants will ensure that relevant information needed to act on their proposals is available." Postponement of a scheduled decision due to the lack of predictably necessary information would constitute a defect. Records may be kept to monitor improvement in conformance, and the additional meeting time required due to defects in the process can be accounted for as a cost of poor quality.

    The following Total Quality principles elaborate on the concepts discussed elsewhere in this handbook. They will improve the effectiveness of any meeting, whether or not your organization is formally involved with Total Quality Management:

- **Identify Significant Variables**
  These variables go beyond setting objectives. They begin with the decision about whether a meeting is the most effective way to meet the need, and include timing, participation guidelines, agenda and other preparation specifications, room arrangements, and anything else that is defined as a significant factor in the success of your meetings.

- **Agree on Criteria**
  Unless everyone involved agrees on the criteria for defining defects, they are hard to enforce and subject to sabotage. Ideally, agreement on criteria is formed by consensus, which generates buy-in, support, and enthusiastic ground rules (see page 66).

- **Define Measurement Method**
  This step gives you a yardstick for measuring conformance to criteria. It lets you know when your process is in need of adjustment.

- **Monitor Conformance to Criteria**
  Use on-going, standardized evaluation to identify defects, or areas where the process doesn't conform to criteria.

- **Eliminate Causes of Defects**
  Defects are often identified during the evaluation process at the end of a meeting. When this happens, schedule time in the next agenda to discuss them. Then use brainstorming and other problem-solving techniques to identify ways to eliminate defects and continually improve the process. Time spent doing this will increase productivity of meetings and effectiveness of meeting results or output.

- **Repeat the Process**
  Keep on identifying defects and eliminating them as long as you find them. Since needs keep changing, you are unlikely to ever find yourself coasting along with nothing to do!

How to Generate Consensus

The process of forming consensus extends participative leadership to its ultimate potential. Decisions made by consensus go beyond soliciting input from the whole group. They are agreed to and supported by every participant. It usually takes longer to arrive at consensus than it does to settle for the majority opinion or invoke executive decision-making privilege. In spite of the time element, consensus is mandatory for lasting and productive agreements on matters of policy and procedure. It is equally important in other instances where all parties must abide by, and actively support, the decision.

Many people confuse consensus with compromise. On the surface they appear similar, because in both cases some people, perhaps all, accept an outcome other than the one they originally sought. The difference is in the perception of the final outcome. In a compromise situation, those who give something up feel a sense of loss. Forming consensus avoids this sense of loss. The process isn't complete until a solution is found that everyone agrees either adequately answers their concerns, or is better than any previous individual proposal. In the end, the willingness to redefine objectives, strategies, and attitudes, creates a sense of gain, and produces demonstrably more effective decisions than those made by any individual.

Bonus results of consensus formation include better decisions and increased team spirit. When individuals have been involved in building consensus, especially on controversial issues, they leave with a sense of personal ownership of the decision and a sense of unity.

People who are not used to the process often find consensus cumbersome. They must resist the temptation to give in and settle for majority rule. At this point, instead of calling for a vote, ask for opinions to emphasize the need for individuals to avoid compromise or giving-in. Use clarification techniques, brainstorming, and other forms of creative problem-solving until a new proposal is found that sincerely satisfies everyone. Problem-solving techniques, such as brainstorming, are important components of the consensus formation process (see pages 146–150). Conflict resolution techniques also help you generate consensus and unblock the process when there is a divergence of opinion (see page 101). The steps below lead you through the process:

- **List Options**
  Record proposed courses of action on a flip chart, chalkboard, paper, or marker board. Collect any previously prepared input at this point (see page 94).

- **Identify Personal Preferences**
  Ask individuals to formulate their own positions.

- **Discuss Options**
  Have individuals clearly explain their positions to the group.

- **Ask For Opinions**
  Have the group begin discussing general preferences and evaluate the merits of various options. Stay focused on constructive input, and avoid killer phrases (see page 105).

The consensus process obviously works best in a trusting atmosphere, with leadership that is committed to empowering subordinates. But lacking that, it must begin somewhere. If your group is tense about some highly politicized issues, people may be unwilling to put personal opinions on the line. A secret poll and discussion of hypothetical reasons why anyone would be against the proposal can be a step toward opening up the channels of communication. This is not to be construed as resorting to voting. The process will still continue until true agreement is reached by all concerned. At some point, the need for the secret polls will almost always disappear.

As conflicting opinions arise, ask the individuals involved to:

- **Restate**
  When conflicting views are expressed, have opposing individuals or groups restate the views of each party for establishing genuine shared understanding of the differences.

- **Rephrase**
  As the discussion continues, each person involved in the controversy will put their own views and concerns in different words until shared understanding is reached.

- **Reconsider**
  Focusing on the actual needs of each party, rather than tradition and personal preference, can lead to novel and innovative ways of addressing these needs.

- **Be Persistent**
  Use creative problem-solving and conflict resolution techniques until shared understanding and synergistic resolution is achieved.

During the consensus-building process, the meeting leader fills the role of facilitator, and must take care not to dominate or interject personal opinion. If the designated meeting leader has a strong opinion or is unskilled in facilitation, appoint another person to facilitate the discussion, or call in an outside facilitator.

Plan-Do-Check-Act

One of the primary purposes for meetings is to solve problems. Some are simple, with obvious solutions. Others can tie up a group for months. Dozens of problem-solving systems are available, ranging in complexity from four simple steps to a dozen or more. Some utilize techniques like story-boarding, which requires only simple materials, and can be effective as well as fun. Others rely on complex computer processes and complicated statistical analytical techniques. Each is appropriate for specific situations, and none is perfect for everything. If you routinely deal with complicated problems, it is worth doing some research on the most effective approach for your specific needs.

Virtually all problems are associated with some process, and the Plan-Do-Check-Act (PDCA) Cycle originally developed by Walter Shewhart is the key to making lasting changes that will reliably improve that process. This cycle involves an ongoing loop of four steps, and can incorporate anything from very simple to the most complex analysis techniques. The PDCA cycle is illustrated and described in Figure 2:

● **PLAN**

– **Understand Process**
Define the process within which the problem occurs, and develop consensus on the shared understanding of this definition.

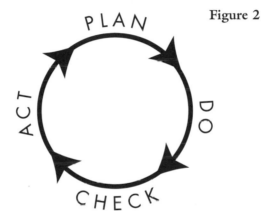

Figure 2

– **Identify and Analyze Root Causes**
There are many tools available, such as Pareto charts, fishbone diagrams, or control charts, to analyze a process and identify the causes of problems. Information about these tools is widely available in books on TQM and Statistical Process Control. Use brainstorming with other appropriate tools to identify possible causes of the problem.

After the possible causes are identified, collect and analyze data, then prioritize causes.

– **Select Solution**
Select the most important cause and develop a proposed solution, along with an action plan for implementing it.

- **DO**

  - **Try It**
    Do a small-scale test of your solution. Collect data on the results.

- **CHECK**

  - **Analyze Results**
    The outcome of the test phase will either verify that the solution is adequate or suggest adjustments that will produce even better results.

  - **Retest**
    If adjustments to the plan are made, do another small-scale test, and repeat this loop until satisfactory results are obtained.

- **ACT**

  - **Implement Procedures**
    Once the results are favorable, standardize and begin using the new procedures system-wide. Continue monitoring results while selecting a new problem and/or cause and repeat the cycle.

Brainstorming Guidelines

The technique of brainstorming is useful at nearly every step of the decision-making process. It can be used to identify multiple causes of problems, decrease the chance that the most significant cause will be overlooked, and generate multiple solutions for each cause. Then it can be used to identify possible solutions and strategies for implementation.

Since the brainstorming term and a general awareness of the technique have been around for decades, many groups use it superficially, but few unleash its real power. There are several reasons why brainstorming is seldom used to full advantage. For instance, most people are ignorant of the extent of the process's potential. They don't know when or how to use it for best results. Also, brainstorming techniques differ from ordinary discussion. To be effective, brainstorming lists must include genuinely wild and radical ideas, and many people find this requirement initially awkward. They don't generally notice that they have reverted to more familiar ideas and behavior and are no longer really brainstorming. Finally, time constraints are a natural enemy of effective and creative brainstorming. People are usually in a hurry.

When you decide to unleash the full power of brain-storming, these basic and unalterable steps, which set it apart from other problem-solving procedures, will be helpful:

1. **Define the Objective**

   Clearly define the objective or problem to be solved. Take some time with this step. Avoid the assumption that your initial perception of the problem is the final focus you should pursue. Your first impression may just be a symptom of a larger, underlying problem. Unless you get to the root of the problem, you will be unable to achieve satisfactory results.

   When you are convinced that you are working on the root cause of your problem, define your desired outcome. Chaos results when people begin brainstorming in all directions without mutual understanding about the desired outcome. However, stay flexible when defining the outcome, and don't be too specific. Sometimes the best solutions are found in forms that would be overlooked if unnecessary restrictions had been imposed on the definition.

2. **Select Your Tools**

   A flip chart and adhesive tape allows sheets to be torn off and kept in view as ideas abound. There are other options. For example, the new electronic marker boards that include a scanner unit to photo copy the surface of the board are especially useful for brainstorming. The standard 8.5" x 11" output of the scanner an be recopied and distributed to participants as a personal record of all ideas. This is especially helpful when the process continues from one session to another, when key people are missing from the group, and when other people or groups need to be kept informed. A portable computer for the recorder is also helpful in making lists of ideas available almost instantly.

Right now, only a few groups have such electronic wonders available, but you don't need to wait for fancy equipment. In a pinch, especially in a very small group, you can even get by with a plain pad of paper and a pencil.

3. **Warm-up**

If your group isn't used to wild and crazy brainstorming, oil their brains by starting with this simple exercise: Choose some small, totally ordinary object, such as a paper clip or a rubber band. Give everyone in the group exactly 120 seconds to work alone, making individual lists of as many alternate uses for the object as they can think of, excluding its obvious, typical use. Go around and collect ideas. In a typical group of 12 people, the number of alternate uses generated by any individual ranges from 2 to 7 (rarely more), with an average of 4.3. The number of unique applications generated by the group of 12 will often exceed 30. They can easily double this number if they build on the first round of ideas with a second round of group brainstorming.

This exercise is fast, fun, and demonstrates the full potential of the process, partly because the item used is so ordinary and unimportant that wild ideas are not threatening.

4. **Write Down Every Idea**

Designate one member as recorder. Traditionally, group members call out ideas as quickly as they can think of them, and as quickly as the recorder can write them on the pad. Some Meeting Masters are getting excellent results by writing individual ideas on Post-It™ notes, which are then posted on any appropriate surface. These are easily rearranged and sorted as part of the evaluation process.

5. **Defer Judgement**

   Write down each idea, without any hint of evaluation. This obviously includes killer phrases (page 105), but you should even avoid encouraging comments or qualifying phrases attached to your own suggestions; for example, avoid "That's a good idea" or "My thought is probably irrelevant, but here it is." Unless you are stating an idea or clarifying one, don't say anything.

6. **Get Crazy**

   The session should be as freewheeling as possible. Each person should voice whatever ideas come to mind, with no holds barred. This is the time to get wild and crazy, bounce off the walls, think like a kid, and speak before you think. In other words, break the rules. You will clean up the mess later. If there are any "stuffy thinkers" among you, make a pact that nothing said will leave the room, and that it is okay to take off your mental corsets among friends! (This should not be construed as condoning insults, rudeness, vulgarity, or anything else damaging to egos and relationships.)

7. **Develop Synergy**

   Build on the ideas of other people. When one person's suggestion sparks an idea for someone else, share it promptly.

8. **Aim for Quantity**

   Quality will be evaluated later. Sometimes the wildest and most unlikely sounding ideas turn out to be the most productive, so don't limit your options.

9. **Analyze the Input**

   Once all the ideas have been collected, it is time to weed them out. Now it is time to use judgment. But don't toss ideas out too quickly. Give them a fair hearing, and prove that they won't work, rather than assuming they won't just because they are different.

   When you have a lot of input that covers several areas, it is helpful to sort it out into an affinity diagram. The affinity diagram clusters information into related areas. For example, during strategic planning sessions brainstorming is used to identify concerns and issues that will affect the future of the business. These concerns are then clustered into an affinity diagram with clusters representing each stakeholder group, i.e., employees, customers, shareholders, management, etc. Items can be placed in more than one cluster.

Several computer programs are available to help develop affinity diagrams and further analyze the data they produce (see page 213).

10. **Make a Decision**
Make a decision about which ideas to use. Tools such as Force Field Analysis (which lists obstacles, or negative forces, in one column and advantages, or positive forces, in the other) can be helpful in making up your mind. Consensus formation may be appropriate (see page 142).

Brainstorming Variations

Dedicated brainstormers have found that you can use brainstorming techniques to improve the brainstorming process itself and identify new ways to brainstorm. Typical reasons for varying from the basic format include time pressure during a meeting, difficulty in convening a group, or simply the need to stay out of a rut.

Examples of alternative formats follow:

● **Remote Location Brainstorming**
Have individuals make independent lists and submit them to a designated recorder who will compile a master list of accumulated suggestions. Then, to spark input before the evaluation process begins, distribute lists of collected ideas. Evaluation can be done as a group, or you can continue the process of circulating compiled input to individuals and collecting further written input. This is most useful when participants are in widely separated locations, making frequent meetings unfeasible, or when the urgency of the need is low.

- **Chinese Auction Brainstorming**
  Begin a list on a clipboard and circulate it, asking each person to write one idea, in turn, while other business or an activity is taking place. Keep the list circulating until everyone runs out of ideas. Since this can be distracting, it is best used in a semi-social situation such as a meal meeting.

- **Round-Robin Brainstorming**
  Divide large groups into smaller ones and have them generate lists. Then circulate each list through the other groups for expansion.

- **Electronic Brainstorming**
  Take advantage of the computer age by designating an e-mail address, or a spot on a computerized bulletin board (see page 180), where people can register and scan ideas on a designated topic. The potential for using this technology is limited only by your imagination.

  Computers can also be useful in brainstorming sessions when used with an LCD projection panel. The recorder, or "technographer," types the ideas into the computer, which projects them onto a screen via the LCD panel. Copies of the list can be printed out to use for evaluating ideas during the meeting or later.

- **Taking Turns**
  This is one way to keep order when a group is large and full of ideas. Provide people with paper and pencil to jot down ideas so they won't be forgotten as new ones arise. Continue around the group until everyone passes for lack of further ideas. Subdividing the group into brainstorming teams to generate initial input also works well.

Fire Fighting Meetings

While it is true that nearly any meeting will become more effective with careful preparation, reality dictates that this is not always possible. We live in an age of crisis management, instantaneous responsiveness, and "just-in-time" operations. "Chinese Fire Drills" are standard operating procedure in many places, and it isn't always feasible to plan a week ahead. In fact, if it weren't for crises, robots and computers could run companies. So perhaps fighting fires is our real work.

If you are summoned to a "Drop Everything" meeting for something like a system failure, or if you ever need to call such a meeting, these guidelines will help you get the best results possible under the circumstances:

- **Hold Off**
  Postpone it as long as possible. Giving people even a few hours notice, instead of expecting immediate response, allows them to gather their thoughts, along with any relevant support material. This may shorten the time necessary to solve the problem and diminish the need for time-consuming follow-up meetings.

- **Keep it Small**
  Spur-of-the-moment meetings are usually problem-solving sessions, requiring lots of spontaneous input for brain storming, etc. Large groups may impede this process.

- **Call in the Experts**
  Include people who have the information or expertise you need to solve the problem.

- **Coach Preparation**
  Let people know what reports or other relevant material they should bring with them.

- **Prepare an Agenda**
  Even a scribbled list of items to be covered is better than nothing. Begin the meeting by clarifying the problem situation and agreeing on what is to be accomplished. Create a plan of action to use as an agenda.

● **Stay Focused**

The stress of the situation may cause this fire to spread to other areas, causing people to jump from one subject to another. Lack of focus leads to feelings of being overwhelmed. Concentrate your own attention and efforts, and, when the discussion wanders, tactfully bring it back to the point.

Planning Informational Meetings

If your group exceeds 50 people, consider using a professional meeting planner to increase its efficiency and effectiveness. If your organization doesn't have a meeting planner on staff, check with the local chapter of Meeting Planners International (see page 213). Large hotels are another source of referrals.

Whether you use a meeting planner or do it yourself, certain considerations are especially important when you are planning a meeting for the purpose of conveying information to a group of people. Use the following checklist to make sure you don't overlook anything:

● **Arrangements**

- Is the room set up appropriately?

- Do you have enough seats, tables, handouts, refreshments, etc.?

- Is it comfortable?

- Can people in the back hear the speaker and see the visuals?

- Is the temperature in the room comfortable?

● **Presentation**

- Is the material well organized?

- Is the material tailored to interests and needs of the audience?

- **Introductions**

  - Who will introduce speaker(s)?

  - Who will serve as moderator?

- **Visual Aids**

  - Can everyone see them clearly?

  - Are they well constructed (see page 124)?

- **Handouts**

  - Are there enough?

  - When will you hand them out?

  - Do you need help to distribute them?

- **Questions**

  - How will you handle them?

  - Do you need any special material for answers?

- **Miscellaneous**

  - Do you need pitchers of water, etc.?

  - Will you be having refreshments, and are they accounted for?

  - Are all supplies in place?

  - Is all equipment available and in working condition?

Planning a Business Meeting

Business meetings may seem like a minor challenge to plan and conduct, because their format is standard, and they can be quite routine. When it seems like you are covering the same list of business, month after month, it may hardly seem worth the effort to plan ahead. But don't be fooled into thinking that just because planning is easy, it is unimportant.

Use these guidelines to follow the standard format for planning, drafting an agenda, and conducting a business meeting:

1. Call to order.

2. Reading and approval of minutes from previous meeting. (If lengthy minutes have been distributed before the meeting, they can be summarized. Or, you can simply ask for questions and corrections.)

3. Reports of officers and standing committees.

4. Reports of special committees.

5. Unfinished business.

6. New business.

7. Program (if planned).

8. Closing comments and adjournment. (Adjournment may precede the program if preferred.)

When you use this outline, add subcategories for officers, committee chairs, and anyone else who will be called upon to report. List scheduled items to be addressed under Unfinished and New Business.

People often try to add new items to the agenda during the meeting. These items may be ideas that just occurred to them, or things they just never got around to mentioning before. If this happens often, the group should address this issue in the ground rules. Ideally, the meeting leader should be contacted with new agenda items far enough ahead to include them on the distributed agenda. This allows everyone time to prepare questions and/or bring relevant information to the meeting. Occasionally an item is sufficiently urgent to justify last minute consideration, and sometimes it's so minor it isn't worth postponing. But more often, this is a sign of ignorance, indifference, or careless preparation. It may even reflect a politically motivated desire to slip something through before most members have had a chance to think about it and voice objections.

Handling Motions

The business of formal organizations, especially those that have some legal jurisdiction, such as governmental bodies, is conducted through the mechanism of motions and voting. If you are involved with a formal organization, especially one that has legal implications for procedure, consult *Robert's Rules of Order*, or an expert on parliamentary procedure. The points listed below will guide you through most everyday meetings that use parliamentary procedure:

- **Wording**
  Motions are formally worded proposals for action or decision by the organization. They are the equivalent of ballot items.

- **Proposing**
  Motions are made by any member other than the meeting chair at any point when a decision is to be made. The chair should clarify the wording for the benefit of both members and the meeting recorder, who includes each motion in the minutes.

- **Seconding**
  Motions must be seconded by another member to be formalized for voting. This "second" is also recorded in the minutes.

- **Discussing**
  After a motion is made, the chair calls for discussion. This can be open or limited. Be aware of the dangers of time limits, as well as their value (see page 90).

- **Amending**
  Amendments to the wording of motions can be made as a subordinate motion, requiring a second, a discussion, and a vote before reconsidering the motion in general.

- **Entertaining**
  Motions can be entertained, but not made, by the chair. If the need for a decision seems apparent and no motion has been made, the chair asks someone to do so by "entertaining a motion to do thus and such."

- **Voting**
  When discussion seems adequate, any member, including the chair, may call for a vote. The formal term is "Question." Voting is generally held by an expression of "yea's" and "nay's," unless a precise count is needed.

- **Withdrawing**
  Motions may be withdrawn from consideration with the agreement of the members who made and seconded the motion.

Working with Volunteers

Volunteer organizations offer special challenges with the multitude of committee and board meetings that they spawn. Members are often extremely busy with professional and personal responsibilities, and board meetings with little personal relevance are near the top of the list of things to eliminate when the calendar is crowded. Yet the charter of the group is such that the meetings are required, and attendance of at least a quorum is necessary to keep the process going. Below are some tips on making these meetings more compelling and manageable for busy professionals.

- **Stay Focused**
  It may seem like extra work for the leader to prepare and distribute the agenda in advance, but this investment of time is usually repaid by time saved in not having to call and nag people to show up or do what they promised. Furthermore, meetings will usually be smoother, shorter, and less stressful for all concerned.

- **Be Lavish with Recognition**
  This may be the only reward for the efforts of these volunteers, so be creative in finding new ways to convey recognition, and don't stint. Thank-you notes, salutes in newsletters, and mentions in meetings are among the most obvious ways of recognizing people. And the easiest of all, a simple "Thank You," is always meaningful, always appropriate, and often left unsaid.

- **Be Flexible**
  Schedule around special needs, i.e., allowing people to come for part of the meeting. Also be flexible in breaking with tradition and rethinking the basic meeting structure. Make your meetings conform to the fundamental purpose of the organization without overwhelming anyone with unnecessary meetings.

- **Recognize Social Needs**
  A certain amount of socializing is the oil that keeps the wheels turning, but don't let it throw you off track. Encourage members to arrive early or stay late to socialize, but stick to business during the actual meeting.

7

Managing Multisite Meetings

Over the past few years, advances in communication and computer technology have shortened the time necessary to complete many tasks – including group tasks. Inevitably, the pace of work is speeding up, shrinking the time windows for making critical decisions.

As a result, a growing number of people are finding it impossible to travel to all the distant meetings they need to attend. And routine meetings within local departments, once the primary vehicle for information and idea sharing, have become costly luxuries.

This reality has made multisite meetings an attractive alternative to traditional, face-to-face meetings. What's more, new technologies are making them increasingly viable and cost effective.

This chapter explores both the features and limitations of various electronic communication mediums and tools, together with tips for using them effectively. Since both hardware and software are rapidly changing, the following discussions will focus on basic descriptions of products and services. General as some of these descriptions are, they should help you in seeking the right information to make sound decisions. For the most up-to-date information on the media and products discussed here, consult computer magazines and the Internet.

Please note that, at this time, many of these tools generally involve sizable investments to implement. Remember, promotional materials supplied by vendors will concentrate entirely on advantages, making it easy to overlook hidden costs, such as those associated with organizational culture and human nature. Be sure to read all promotional materials very carefully and with your organization in mind.

Multisite Meeting Strategies

Multisite meetings can save significant time and money by eliminating the cost and inconvenience of travel. Because of this important advantage, the costs associated with a multisite meeting are often insignificant compared to the savings; however, you should select your medium carefully.

As you move up the ladder from teleconferencing using individual desk phones, to linked conference rooms, to group video conferencing with shared application software, costs can escalate. And the additional features don't always add significant value. (Sometimes the technological limitations of a medium are even counter-productive, especially when equipment doesn't work as expected. This is even a consideration, though less so, when working with a professional service provider. If you invest in your own equipment, make sure you become as familiar as possible with it, so you can effectively troubleshoot, when necessary.)

When you do decide to schedule a multisite meeting, remember that all of the rules for face-to-face meetings still apply. With the additional cost of equipment and phone lines, it becomes even more critical that all participants are prepared, that the discussion is kept tightly focused, and that decisions and assignments are clearly communicated to everyone. All tips in earlier sections on clarifying purpose (page 68), preparing agendas (page 43), using ground rules (page 66), and managing discussions (page 85) will be helpful in multisite meetings.

Helpful Hint

If you schedule a meeting that will involve participants from across a large geographical area, be mindful of time zones. When intercontinental sites are involved, avoid misunderstandings by specifying times in Greenwich Mean Time (GMT) as well as local times (see page 161).

Greenwich Mean Time (GMT) Conversion Table

GMT -12:00	Eniwetok, Kwajalein
GMT -11:00	Midway Island, Samoa
GMT -10:00	Hawaii
GMT -09:00	Alaska
GMT -08:00	Pacific Time (US & Canada); Tijuana
GMT -07:00	Mountain Time (US & Canada), Arizona
GMT -06:00	Central Time (US & Canada), Saskatchewan, Mexico City, Tegucigalpa
GMT -05:00	Eastern Time (US & Canada), Indiana (east), Bogota, Lima
GMT -04:00	Atlantic Time (Canada), Caracas, La Paz
GMT -03:30	Newfoundland
GMT -03:00	Brasilia, Buenos Aires, Georgetown
GMT -02:00	Mid-Atlantic
GMT -01:00	Azores, Cape Verde Islands
GMT 00:00	Dublin, Edinburgh, London, Monrovia, Casablanca
GMT +01:00	Lisbon, Madrid, Stockholm, Amsterdam, Paris, Bern, Brussels, Berlin, Warsaw, Vienna, Prague, Rome
GMT +02:00	Eastern Europe, Athens, Helsinki, Istanbul, Israel, Cairo, Harare, Pretoria,
GMT +03:00	St. Petersburg, Moscow, Baghdad, Riyadh, Kuwait, Nairobi
GMT +03:30	Tehran
GMT +04:00	Tbilisi, Kazan, Volgograd, Abu Dhabi, Muscat
GMT +04:30	Kabul
GMT +05:00	Ekaterinburg, Tashkent, Islamabad, Karachi
GMT +05:30	Bombay, Calcutta, Madras, New Delhi, Colombo
GMT +06:00	Almaty, Dhaka
GMT +07:00	Bangkok, Jakarta, Hanoi

Greenwich Mean Time (GMT) Conversion Table (cont.)

GMT +08:00	Beijing, Chongqing, Urumqi, Hong Kong, Taipei, Singapore
GMT +09:00	Yakutsk, Seoul, Tokyo, Osaka, Sapporo
GMT +09:30	Adelaide, Darwin
GMT +10:00	Vladivostok, Guam, Port Moresby, Brisbane, Melbourne, Sydney, Hobart
GMT +11:00	Magadan, Solomon Islands, New Caledonia
GMT +12:00	Kamchatka, Fiji, Marshall Islands, Wellington, Auckland

To use this table, select the time you wish to schedule an event in your home time zone. Consult the table to determine how many hours to add or subtract from your home time zone to express it in GMT. If your home time zone is expressed as a negative number, i.e. -06:00 for the United States Central Time Zone, it will be six hours later in the day in the Greenwich Time Zone. If you want to schedule an event at 8 a.m. (08:00) in the Central Time Zone in the United States, the time expressed in GMT is 8:00 + 6 hours, or 2:00 p.m., (14:00) GMT. In time zones to the east of the Greenwich Time Zone, the time is later in the day, so you add the appropriate number of hours to GMT. For example, 2:00 p.m. or 14:00 GMT is 23:00, or 11:00 p.m. in Tokyo.

Video Conferencing

The basic technology for video conferencing has been around for years, but high costs and low quality have limited its use. Now prices are dropping and technology is improving. As a result, many organizations are installing their own video conferencing facilities to save time and money, and speed up decision making. Many other organizations, meanwhile, are making use of the growing number of commercial video conferencing facilities, giving them access to this important technology without making a major capital investment.

Currently, most video conferencing is done with dedicated equipment, installed in specially-equipped rooms or on mobile carts. The cost of equipping a video conferencing room can easily zoom past $50,000; mobile equipment is significantly less expensive.

Video cameras mounted on personal computers are an increasingly popular option. These systems, which can be installed for a few hundred dollars each, allow a person to see faces when making phone calls. Soon, video conferencing service providers will be able to simultaneously display live individual images of several meeting participants on a standard computer monitor. This means you will be able to sit at your desk and see the reactions of each person in the meeting, perhaps more closely than you might while sitting around a table in an actual meeting room.

Several issues are involved in the decision to hold a video conference. One is cost. Some costs will be incurred in any meeting, whether it's a face-to-face meeting held in one room, or a video conference linking participants at multiple sites. These costs can be calculated with the Meeting Cost Calculator on page 25. The following Video Conference Cost Calculator, which compares the special costs associated with multisite video conferences with single-site meetings requiring travel, will help you determine whether scheduling a video conference is a good investment.

Video Conference Cost Calculator

Fixed Costs		
a. Total travel time involved to attend meeting (include all participants in figure)		
b. Hourly cost of travel time		
c. Total cost of travel time (a x b)		
d. Other travel costs (airfare, hotels, etc.)		
e. Misc. costs (conference room, meals, etc.)		
f. **Total cost of convening meeting** (c + d + e)		
Rental Option		
g. Cost of renting video conference facilities		
h. Misc. costs (local travel, etc.)		
i. **Total cost of video conference** (f + g + h)		
Owned Equipment Option		
j. Phone line costs		
k. Bridging service (if required)		
l. **Total cost of video conference** (f + j + k)		

Other considerations for the use of video include convenience, scheduling issues, and the overall effect on communication. Many companies have found that maintaining a conference room with a constant live link between remote sites is a cost-effective way to improve and energize communication between those sites.

Consider your purpose carefully when deciding whether or not to use video conferencing, especially for a multisite event. If a group is too large for personal interaction in a face-to-face situation, a video conference won't make the event feel more intimate. However, when there is an urgent need to have a live speaker share a specific, time-sensitive message across a wide arena in real time, video conferencing can be the best option. (In less urgent situations, a videotape of the speaker may serve the purpose just as well. This alternative will likely be cheaper, more convenient and serve to convey the message just as effectively.)

Whether you use video conferencing every day, or only occasionally, the following tips will help you prepare for a productive video conference:

- **Know the Site**
  If you've never used the room or site, be sure to visit it a day or more beforehand to familiarize yourself with the equipment, plan the seating arrangement and work out the placement of any visual aids.

- **Give Clothing Suggestions**
  Include clothing suggestions with the agenda for the benefit of those who may be unfamiliar with this protocol.

- **Advance Distribution**
  Be sure everyone has a copy of the agenda and any handouts or other necessary materials before the video connection is made.

- **Plan Camera Position**
  Ensure that each person in your group can be seen clearly. Change the camera position frequently to keep everyone energized and interested.

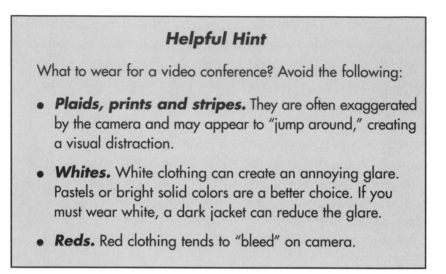

Helpful Hint

What to wear for a video conference? Avoid the following:

- **Plaids, prints and stripes.** They are often exaggerated by the camera and may appear to "jump around," creating a visual distraction.

- **Whites.** White clothing can create an annoying glare. Pastels or bright solid colors are a better choice. If you must wear white, a dark jacket can reduce the glare.

- **Reds.** Red clothing tends to "bleed" on camera.

Using Supporting Visuals

Many video systems allow you to cut to shots of supporting materials such as objects, printed materials, or presentation graphics fed in from a computer. Electronic slide presentations, such as those created in Powerpoint, simple spreadsheets, maps, graphs, and similar visual aids work well as supporting visuals. If planning to use any of these materials, consult your video specialist for help in utilizing them for maximum effectiveness. If using overheads or slide presentations, note the tips below as well as those listed on page 124.

Helpful Hint

- Black text is the most visible for overheads and slide presentations used in video conferencing.

- Save bright colors like orange, red and yellow for highlighting points.

- Try to maintain a balance between "face time" and visuals to preserve the feel of a meeting, as opposed to an informational video.

Once the initial novelty wears off, a video conference feels almost as natural as a meeting held in a single office or conference room. The following tips on video conferencing protocol will help speed up this eventuality:

- **Emphasize Introductions**
  Even if people have met before, they may not immediately recognize each other on video, especially if a group is on camera. Use clearly visible tent cards for each person, listing both the participant's name and the site where he or she is located. Introduce all participants at each site.

- **Allow for the Time Lag**
  Video signals often incur a slight transmission delay. To account for this, keep your statements concise and stop periodically to allow those at other sites a chance to respond to questions or comments.

- **Keep Everyone Informed**
  Let people know when you are about to switch modes, i.e., show a slide or another visual. This will prevent multiple sites from trying to switch to graphics at the same time – which can result in chaos.

- **Track the Camera**
  If you switch cameras to show a graphic, remember to switch it back to the table when discussion resumes. When more than one camera is focused on the table, speak to the live one.

- **Be Yourself**
  Use a natural voice and imagine that people at other sites are sitting across the table from you, not across town or around the globe. Remember, looking directly into the camera is just like looking directly into the eyes of your listeners. Think of the camera lens as a big eye smiling back at you.

- **Avoid Noise and Other Distractions**
  Ensure that all cellular phones and beepers are off, and that a "Do Not Disturb" sign is posted on the door. Caution everyone about coughing into microphones, tapping fingers, shuffling papers, or whispering to others.

- **Be Conscious of Time**
  Aside from issues of cost, this is especially important when using a commercial facility or a busy conference room when others may be waiting. Be prepared, be organized, and be on time.

Conducting Effective Multisite Video Conferences

When more than two sites are involved, use of a multipoint switcher is required. This voice-activated device changes the on-screen image to show the site that is currently talking.

The necessity of using one of these switchers presents an extra challenge to conducting a successful multisite video conference, as total chaos can result if participants at two or more sites try to talk at the same time.

However, this challenge, and many others, can be overcome by heeding the following tips for conducting smooth and effective multisite conferences:

- **Designate Site Leaders**
  The meeting leader at the master site should convene the meeting and coordinate the overall session. Each additional site should also have a site leader to control equipment and facilitate off-camera interaction. Determine ahead of time whether sites will enter the discussion spontaneously, or on cue from the master site leader.

- **Emphasize Introductions**
  Begin the meeting by introducing every participant at every site, including anyone out of camera range.

- **Use the Mute Button**
  Each site should make use of the mute button, to keep microphones inactive until participants are ready to be seen and heard.

- **Don't Rush**
  Allow the on-screen site to finish talking before you respond. The multiswitch jumps wildly back and forth when more than one person speaks, creating visual pandemonium.

Voice Conferencing

Teleconference calls multiply the convenience and time saving advantages of two-party calls. Because they can be conducted without leaving the office, they eliminate time and travel costs and may be the only feasible way to make a live connection among remote sites. The simplest form, adding a third party to a call between two people, is now a very common feature that is routinely available even to residential customers. The easy access to this medium lets most anyone initiate third-party calls, even on the spur of the moment. However, even these simple calls are a form of meeting. And as with any meeting, a little advance planning to set objectives for the conversation will save time and improve results.

For more structured conference calls, you can engage a voice conferencing service provider. Many long distance phone companies provide this conference call service. Taking into account operator fees, bridging service (required if more than two sites will be participating) and applicable long distance charges, careful planning and attention to ground rules can help you save a significant amount of money.

The following table will help you identify special costs inherent to a teleconference versus those associated with a single-site, face-to-face meeting:

Voice Conference Cost Calculator

	Single-Site Meeting Costs		
a.	Total travel time involved to attend meeting (include all participants in total)		
b.	Hourly cost of travel time		
c.	Total cost of travel time (a x b)		
d.	Other travel costs (airfare, hotels, etc.)		
e.	Misc. costs (conference room, meals, etc.)		
f.	Total cost of single-site meeting (c + d + e)		
	Teleconference		
g.	Phone line costs		
h.	Bridging service (required if more than two sites are involved)		
i.	Total operating cost of teleconference (g +h)		

The following tips will help you plan a smooth voice conference:

● **Schedule Service and Facilities**
  If a group is to share a phone during the call, reserve a conference room and a speakerphone. Find the best speaker phone you can afford to buy, rent or borrow. Simple desk-model speakerphones do not provide high-quality service, and are inadequate for groups.

Contact your service provider or corporate teleconferencing bridge manager and schedule the call. If, for some reason, the conference call is canceled, you will want to notify your service provider as soon as possible to avoid "no-show" fees.

● **Learn How to Use the Service**
When you schedule the call, find out how to signal the operator for assistance and how to use any special features that participants will use, such as phone balloting. Include any relevant equipment instructions with the agenda.

● **Ask Participants to be Early**
When you use a service provider, include with the agenda a request that all participants be at their phones at least ten minutes before the scheduled starting time to assist the operator in setting up the call. For calls that merely require dialing a bridge access number, make sure everyone knows the number.

● **Test Transmission Quality**
Test the quality of the audio transmission shortly before the call begins, especially when using speakerphones.

● **Choose Equipment Carefully**
Speakerphones that echo or offer poor transmission quality can increase the stress level of a voice conference. It is especially important to use equipment with good directional capabilities if the groups will be sitting around a table.

Use the following tips during the call to maintain focus and realize best results:

● **Mute Speakerphones**
Ask participants who are using speakerphones to mute them when they are not speaking. Unexpected noises, such as chair squeaks or dropped pens, can divert the microphone – and the attention of all participants – from the person speaking.

- **Don't Put the Call on Hold**
  The whole conference call can be disrupted if a call goes on hold and music or advertisements begin to play.

- **Speak Clearly**
  Ask participants to use their natural "phone voices," speaking clearly and naturally, without yelling.

- **Identify Speakers**
  Unless only three or four people who are well-acquainted will be participating, ask each participant to state his or her name each time before speaking.

- **Signal Entrances and Exits**
  When joining a teleconference in mid-session, announce your presence at the earliest opportunity, being careful not to interrupt anyone. Likewise, excuse yourself before hanging up if the meeting isn't over and you must disconnect.

- **Clarify Follow-Up**
  Schedule any necessary follow-up calls while everyone is on the line. This will save time and eliminate confusion.

As technology advances, additional teleconferencing options and features become available. Some of the options currently provided by voice conferencing service providers include:

- **Flexible Scheduling**
  Service provider operators can conveniently connect specific participants for only the part of the conference call that involves them. For example, the operator can seamlessly handle the details of getting an attorney on the line for ten minutes to discuss a specific issue, without distracting other participants.

- **Breakout Discussions**
  If you have several lines connected on one call, the operator can cluster them into separate "virtual rooms" for a period

of time. This allows two or more groups to hold simultaneous mini-conferences. The operator can toggle back and forth from these clusters to the larger group without having to restart the whole calling process.

- **Balloting**
  Many providers offer a balloting option so that participants can vote on issues by pressing designated phone keys. The results are tallied electronically, and conveyed by the operator to the meeting leader. Balloting conducted this way is confidential, so that during the meeting, nobody knows how anyone else voted. This anonymity may encourage a deeper level of honesty in groups where some people are reluctant to publicly disagree. A printout of the results is available to the meeting leader after the teleconference.

Shared Application Software

Although shared application software is relatively new to most organizations, it is proving to be an extremely useful tool for two or more people to work together. These packages allow individuals using computers linked by modems to work interactively on files, using any software program installed on, or accessible to, the host machine. The active program is also accessible through the guest computer – even if it is not installed on the guest computer's hard drive – allowing another individual to work on the file. In addition to the phone line linking the modems, a second line is used for a voice link among those working on files together. When the session ends, the application disappears from the screen of the guest computer, and all work is saved to disk or the hard drive on the host computer.

Shared application packages also can be invaluable resources for video conferences, whether they are conducted between groups in conference rooms, or between desktop units. Linking more than two or three computers requires a voice conferencing bridge (see page 169); consult the software vendor for specific hardware requirements when using video.

Among the benefits of shared application software:

- **Improved Task Focus**
  When participants at multiple sites have access to the same documents, spreadsheets or other computer files, the result can be a shared focus that keeps the discussion on track.

- **Expanded Resource Base**
  If additional information, in the form of a computer file, is needed. It can be accessed by more than one computer relatively quickly.

- **Faster Turnaround**
  When a group works collectively to make changes to a document, design or proposal, it may be possible to bypass circulating it for review and feedback.

- **Decreased Conflict**
  Working together on computer in real time can help to eliminate memory discrepancies that often pop up afterward. Likewise, the ability to share facts and figures on-screen allows for discussion on the spot and prevents misunderstandings.

The following tips will help you realize the greatest benefit from shared application packages:

- **Choose a Facilitator**
  Designate one person to take the lead in the keying in of information. Cursor movement activates the system much like voice-activated microphones and cameras. In fact, the system may crash if two people try to make entries at the same time. All participants should seek clearance from the facilitator before typing in anything.

- **Be Selective**
  Only include those people whose input is relevant.

- **Keep Track of All Participants**
  The facilitator should make sure everyone is actively involved. This is especially important when one person has taken charge for an extended period of time.

Shared Site Whiteboards

The ubiquitous whiteboard has been electronically enhanced to allow you to save notes and drawings, and share them between sites. The simplest units run a continuous loop of flexible white-board surface through a scanner unit. More sophisticated units, meanwhile, function as a 67-inch computer monitor and use space-age technology to offer a wide range of capabilities.

Regardless of the level of sophistication, using one of these boards will help focus your meeting on the task at hand and increase the amount of real work that gets done. The benefits of different levels of sophistication and their merits are discussed below.

No special guidelines beyond those given in the shared application software, video conferencing and voice conferencing sections are necessary for using these boards. In spite of the dazzling technology, meetings in which these boards are utilized should be approached no differently than any other meeting.

Scanner Boards

These boards have a scanner unit that transfers images written on the board surface to a standard 8½" x 11" sheet of paper. The most basic scanner boards utilize a printer unit, mounted at the base of the board, which provides the hard copy on thermal paper. On more sophisticated models, the scanner is connected to a fax modem, allowing for transmission of the image to a remote location, or for saving it as a bitmap computer file.

Computer Interfaced Boards

Boards are available that convert words and diagrams drawn on the surface into computer files that can be saved to disk, printed out, and transmitted to remote sites. The type of marker used varies from one manufacturer to another, but all come in at least four colors.

A computer-linked projection device displays files on the board, providing a background for additional input with the markers. The board is designed to transmit all marker input back to the computer to be saved, complete with color, as a graphics file.

With the addition of shared application software, you can link multiple sites for brainstorming or group problem-solving sessions. If your video conference signal is transmitted through a computer, it can be projected onto one of these boards as a full-size image or displayed in a small window visible over a running application.

Software Interactive Boards

The most sophisticated electronic white boards are similar to huge video units, providing the best meeting support technologies in one package. These 67-inch computer monitors also work like a traditional whiteboard, accommodating laser pens with multiple colors and cursor shapes. These pens perform all mouse functions and register on the screen from a distance of several feet. A handwriting recognition feature allows an individual to make handwritten corrections to a document. These corrections are instantly converted to type. (When linked through modems to personal computers, remote sites can monitor and participate in the meeting by using keyboards instead of laser pens.)

The boards are computer driven and can serve as network clients, so any software program can be called up for instant access to data, text or graphics. Many offer multimedia and video capabilities, so the screen can be used for presentations and video conferencing.

Summary of Shared Site Whiteboard Features

Features	*Scanner Board*	*Computer Interface*	*Software Interactive*
Hard copy of collected ideas provides accurate record	X	X	X
Record immediately available for copying and distribution	X	X	X
Works with POTS lines	X	X	X
Fax/modem unit allows rapid exchange of information with other sites	X	X	X
Records color input		X	X
Keyboard input possible		X	X
Can be linked by modem with standard computer terminals		X	X
Can display video conferencing images on full screen or in reduced-size window		X	X
Facilitates group involvement with shared application software		X	X
On-screen changes to actual application prevents current and future misunderstanding			X
Laser pens provide control program interaction, even from a distance			X
Handwriting recognition capability			X
Automatic spacing adjustment when handwritten lists are rearranged			X
Unique cursor color and shape can be assigned to each linked site for instant identification			X

8

Software Tools for Managing Meetings

Announcements appear in the media almost daily about some
new piece of software or high-tech tool that promises to make
every meeting more productive and cost-effective. Wiping away
the hype, what's encouraging about many of these products is
how they allow you to get more out of the standard computer
system you probably already use.

The most exciting, and most promising applications enable
you to hold "virtual meetings," allowing people to work together
and interact without meeting face-to-face. This strategy can save
enormous amounts of time and money, and often improves
results. Other software packages add impact to traditional
"meetings as we have always known them" by making it easier
to schedule meeting times, put together agendas, create attractive
presentations, facilitate discussions, help groups solve problems
and generate workable solutions.

This chapter explores the benefits and limitations of several
types of software tools for managing meetings, and provides tips
for using them effectively.

Helpful Hint

To find the most current information on software, check
software magazines and the Internet. Use one of the many
search engines on the World Wide Web to locate information, demonstration software and shareware. Examples of
typical search strings are "multi-voting systems," "group
decision-making," or "facilitation software." Many software
companies allow you to download demonstration versions of
their software from their Web sites, giving you the opportunity to try before you buy.

Helpful Hint

Total Quality, process improvement and management consultants often use and recommend problem-solving/decision-support software. You may want to tap these professionals for their knowledge on various products. Just remember, however, that they have a vested interest in the product or service they represent.

Virtual Meetings

Even with all the electronic enhancements available to streamline meetings and improve their results, in the future, the number of meetings you actually attend will probably drop. Software engineers have been working for years to develop "groupware," the equivalent of electronic bulletin boards, that are versatile enough to allow people to collaborate on projects without having face-to-face meetings. Early versions of these programs were expensive and often awkward to use. Furthermore, outside consultants were required to install them, maintain them, and teach people how to use them.

As the World Wide Web has mushroomed, something exciting has happened. Web-like internal networks called "Intranets" have developed, allowing individuals and groups to tap all sorts of previously inaccessible information. Unlike the Internet, Intranets are secure, closed, internal systems. The fact that both use the same basic communication technology has enabled the development of a whole new line of groupware products to support bulletin board-style discussion groups. These discussion groups permit people to check in now and then, read what others are saying about a question, topic or problem, and add their own thoughts. Benefits include:

- **Freedom from Meetings**
  A great deal of information, such as status reports or routine updates, can be transmitted without the need for face-to-face

meetings. As a result, time that was formerly spent in irrelevant meetings can now be spent scanning the Intranet to stay informed.

● **Time Flexibility**
People can read and respond to topics at their convenience. Information exchanged this way is often done so more efficiently and rapidly than by scheduling a meeting.

● **Selective Attention**
People can read and respond to items of relevance and interest, and ignore the rest.

● **Broadened Information Base**
Although sensitive discussion areas can be limited with passwords, broad, general access enables interested individuals to gain a wider perspective on the organization and increase the reach and value of their contributions.

● **Personal Responsiveness**
E-mail options are included in many programs to allow responses to be sent directly to an individual, as opposed to posting them to the whole Intranet.

● **Geographic Diversity**
Groupware enables teams to function across boundaries of time and space. This is especially valuable in intercontinental collaboration.

● **Participation Becomes More Spontaneous**
Many people find it easier to express their thoughts in writing instead of risking exposing their feelings verbally to a group.

● **Tempers are Less Likely to Flare**
With time to think before replying, volatile statements can be avoided.

In addition to the many benefits of Intranet discussion groups, other factors should be taken into account:

- **Keyboarding Skills are Critical**
  Hunt-and-peck typists will have difficulty participating in this forum.

- **Writing Skills Matter**
  Some people are more articulate than others at conveying a message in writing.

- **Training and Support are Imperative**
  People are often reluctant to take the time to explore and learn new things on their own, especially when they are under intense time pressure.

- **Groupware can be Impersonal**
  People want to maintain a sense of personal contact in the face of electronic communication and are reluctant to completely abandon face-to-face meetings.

- **Postings and E-mails may be Inflammatory**
  Many people dash off replies to e-mail and groupware postings without thinking things through. Bluntness and failing to provide a context can cause or exacerbate conflict. Remember, feelings can be hurt over an e-mail or posting just as they can be in a face-to-face exchange. Likewise, when reading electronic messages, give people the benefit of the doubt before going up in smoke. Clarify meaning and context as soon as possible, preferable by phone or in person.

Use the following tips for best results with groupware:

- **Define "Netiquette"**
  Develop a set of ground rules for using the system. For example, TYPING IN ALL CAPS is called "shouting" and should be

discouraged. You should also discourage abusive, negative language, and define guidelines for reasonable maximum length of posted items. Post Netiquette ground rules on-line now and then, and send gentle e-mail reminders to offenders.

- **Provide Support**
  In addition to providing training on using the software, give people the help they need to improve typing and writing skills, as well. Benefits from improving these skills will far exceed training costs.

Scheduling

A master calendar program showing your entire staff's schedule can save hours or even days of phone tag or e-mail exchanges. Many Personal Information Manager (PIM) software packages are available in groupware form for use on networks. These packages automatically update the master calendar as individuals update their own.

To get the most out of group scheduling software:

- **Provide Training on Use of the Program**
  People naturally avoid using something unfamiliar. Make sure everyone understands the benefits of the software, how to use it, and why it is important for everyone to utilize it.

- **Get Everyone's Commitment to Use the Program**
  Group calendar systems only work if everyone keeps the system up to date. Impulsive individuals are temperamentally unsuited to this degree of structure and accountability, and may drag their heels on compliance. The best way to get their commitment is to include them in the decision to select and implement the system.

● **Double-Check Plans**
Don't take it for granted that information is perfectly up-to-date at any given time. Always ask for verification of dates and times before finalizing meeting times or other plans.

Agenda Preparation

The most basic preparation software is a word processing package. Recent versions of the most popular ones, such as Word® or WordPerfect®, include templates or wizards that guide you through the process of putting together an agenda. If you have one of these templates available, take a few minutes with the help screens to learn how to customize it for your own needs. If you are using an older version of a program that doesn't include templates, you can realize the same benefits by setting up a blank document in the format you want and filling it in each time you need an agenda. Make sure to save it with a new filename each time to keep your "template" intact. However you utilize them, templates will save time and ensure uniform and complete information (see pages 43–50 for further information on customizing agendas).

Meeting facilitation software packages also include agenda templates of varying degrees of sophistication. This feature can be helpful even if you don't use the rest of the program functions.

Presentation Software

Presentation packages, such as Microsoft® PowerPoint, Lotus FreeLance Graphics®, or Corel Presentations™, are typically bundled with office suite packages, and are affordable add-ons if you don't already have them. They are invaluable time savers when preparing presentations, and provide an easy way to add impact to your message.

Unfortunately, many people continue to photocopy deadly dull pages of text, bulleted lists and spreadsheets onto overhead transparencies, distributing the identical material as handouts. If you have one of these packages, learn to use it. If you ever use overheads and don't have a presentation software package, invest in one. When using one of these programs, follow basic guidelines for preparing overhead transparencies (see page 124). Additional tips on using presentation software follow:

● **Use Graphics**
Replace bulleted lists with graphs, charts, or other illustrations whenever possible. For example, consider the difference in impact between Figure 1 and Figure 2.

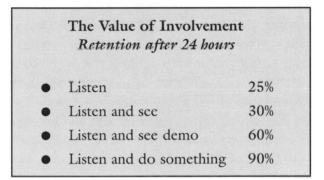

The Value of Involvement
Retention after 24 hours

● Listen   25%
● Listen and see   30%
● Listen and see demo   60%
● Listen and do something   90%

Figure 1

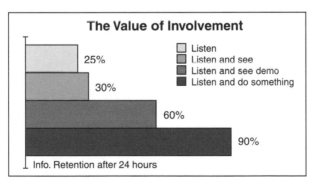

The Value of Involvement

25%
30%
60%
90%

☐ Listen
▨ Listen and see
▨ Listen and see demo
■ Listen and do something

Info. Retention after 24 hours

Figure 2

● **Use a Template**
Select an appropriate background template to unify your presentation and focus viewers on your message. Match the background to the purpose, sticking with a simple background for complex information.

- **Use Color**
  Color adds impact to your slides, but don't overdo it. Stick to two or three colors and use a pale background with dark text. Dark backgrounds are like a light-absorbing sponge, especially when you are working with electronically projected slides. If you keep the background light, you can often avoid dimming room lights.

Once they have a presentation software package, many people choose to create projected presentations rather than opting for overheads. This makes it a snap to customize presentations and add last-minute slides. This step also allows you to further enhance your slides with animation, sound effects and other attention-getting devices. Newer versions of the software allow you to embed hyperlinks to jump from one slide to another, or to other applications such as spreadsheets, by simply clicking on designated areas of the slide.

When you take advantage of such bells and whistles, think carefully about where the focus of the audience will be. If you want to remain the center of attention, keep your visual aids low-key and use the manual advance option to move from slide to slide. If you want the show to speak for itself, you can make it do that, too.

Facilitation Software

Facilitation software includes features for managing the meeting process. The simplest program merely projects a timer onto a screen to emphasize the amount of time spent on different issues. More elaborate packages work like electronic flipcharts. As the discussion proceeds, one individual makes notes on a computer, which are projected onto a screen as they are typed. These packages generally include modules with simple problem-solving tools, which are discussed in the next section.

The projection equipment needed to use these programs is also useful for making presentations, conducting training, and working with electronic whiteboards. If you would use facilitation software frequently for these other purposes, it could prove to be a worthwhile purchase. Otherwise, think seriously about making the investment for the sole purpose of running meetings.

Requirements for using these packages include:

- **Computer**

  A notebook computer that can be carried to conference rooms is the most convenient choice. Small groups may find it satisfactory to meet around a desktop unit with a monitor large enough for all to read.

- **Projection Unit**

  This may be a liquid crystal display (LCD) projection unit that is used with an extra-bright overhead projector, or a projector unit with its own light source. Another option is an electronic white board (see page 175).

- **Software**

  Although special programs are on the market to organize your meeting efforts, a word processing program will do the job. It just doesn't have the bells and whistles such as charting and brainstorming components.

- **Technographer**

  This is the high tech name for a scribe. The technographer sits at the keyboard and records the notes for all to see. This person should be able to type accurately and quickly to avoid creating distractions or slowing the discussion.

- **Facilitator**

  Since the technographer must concentrate on operating the software, which may involve toggling from screen to screen while entering information, a facilitator is needed to direct the discussion and clarify any content. Use standard meeting facilitation guidelines (see page 58).

Using projection equipment to assist the meeting facilitator has obvious benefits, but there are also other considerations. A summary of both follows:

Benefits	Other Considerations
• Group attention is focused more on the screen, and thus the issues, and less on personalities.	• Most projectors work best in a darkened room. This makes it more difficult for participants to see each other and to keep their own notes.
• Everyone sees the information, so disagreements can be resolved immediately.	• Only a limited amount of information can be displayed at one time. Taking time to print out lists and distribute them during the meeting is time-consuming and cumbersome.
• The meeting record is immediately available for printing and distribution at the end of the meeting, or even sooner.	• It may be difficult to find a technographer with good keyboarding skills.
• The file is stored, and readily available for reference.	• The technographer needs to be trained on the software before using it with the group.
	• The group may become distracted by the wording of the record and lose sight of the larger issue.
	• There is no provision for using this equipment with breakout groups.

The obvious alternative to using this software is the traditional flipchart or whiteboard. Flipcharts are still preferred by many, because the pages can be taped up around the room, forming a readily available memory tool for the group.

Problem-Solving/Decision-Support Software

This category covers a wide variety of programs. Simple problem-solving tools like brainstorming, affinity diagrams, fishbone diagrams or Pareto charts are generally included with facilitation packages. More elaborate programs are available for specific applications like mind-mapping or flow-charting. Decision-making tools, like programs based on the Analytic Hierarchy Process (see page 213), can reduce confusion and slash time involved in making complicated decisions. Multi-voting systems introduce electronic gadgets similar to remote controls which participants use to express preferences or vote anonymously on issues.

Unless the issues are highly complex, most problem-solving activities can be done as well and sometimes faster with simple tools like Post-It™ Notes and flipcharts (see page 125). Transforming this information into a form that can be distributed may be slow, and presents the opportunity for inaccuracies. Software tools may save time and improve communication by organizing information so that it can be printed out and copied on the spot. As an additional benefit, you can use the computer files created during the meeting for subsequent purposes.

The advantages and challenges of problem-solving/decision-support software and systems are similar to those listed in the previous section on facilitation software. The main difference is the distraction factor. While solving problems, the group will typically focus on a whiteboard, flipchart sheets, etc., not on each other. Projected images are less distracting for groups working on solving problems and making data-based decisions than they are in ordinary discussions.

Use the following tips to ensure success if you do decide to go high-tech:

- **Skilled Facilitator**

  The skill of the facilitator is always a major key to success, but it is not safe to assume that a facilitator who excels at using traditional methods will automatically know how to use the latest technology. Make sure your facilitator is trained in the specific process you select. The more elaborate the process and software, the more extensive this training should be.

- **Skilled Technographer**

  Select a technographer who is well-trained and competent at using the software. Fumbling with the program, or constantly correcting mistakes, is distracting.

- **Powerful Computer**

  Use a computer with enough power to run the software quickly. Few things are as distracting and irritating to a group as waiting a minute or more while an image loads from a disk.

9

Summary

No two meetings are alike. Even when you meet with the same group over a period of time, each meeting will be different. The content will change, the moods and motivation of participants will vary, and pressures external to the group will fluctuate. This variation may seem like an irritating factor to those who are trying to get uniformly good results from meetings. It does pose an extra challenge. But it can also be viewed in a positive light. Think how dreadfully boring they would be if they always stayed the same! As often as not, the variation can be used to advantage by those who anticipate it and are ready to capitalize on it.

The material in the previous sections provides tools for building on natural variation to stimulate change and make your meetings more productive and effective. Key concepts are summarized below:

● **Meetings are costly.**
The one resource shared by every person and every business is time. We all have it in equal measure. One of the biggest factors in achieving success is the ability to use it wisely.

Meetings pose a special challenge in using time wisely. Since business, by definition, involves transactions between two or more people, nobody can conduct business without participating in meetings of some sort upon occasion. Time spent in meetings is an investment, and like any investment, it should be made and managed wisely. Don't schedule or attend meetings unless they will provide some tangible benefit for you.

Beyond the personal level, meetings have the potential to be a major time trap for groups, because the collective amount of time wasted by inefficient meetings grows

191

exponentially as the size of the group increases. Therefore, any investment in reducing the amount of time required to conduct the meetings, and/or in making the process more productive and effective, will yield tremendous dividends.

- **Planning and Preparation pay large dividends.**
  One of the most effective strategies for making meetings more productive is planning and preparation. This process involves clarifying the objectives for outcomes of the meeting, negotiating an agreeable time and place with selected participants, obtaining preliminary input from those who will be involved, clarifying the roles each will play during the meeting (including necessary preparation on their part), drafting and distributing an appropriate agenda, and making any necessary arrangements for a place and equipment.

  Planning should be done in proportion to the strategic importance of the meeting and the number of people who will be attending. Obviously, a brief update meeting involving only one or two other people will not require extensive preparation. Much more thought is necessary for major internal meetings, such as strategic planning sessions or Quality Council meetings. Meetings involving other groups, for example soliciting customer input for a new product, or presenting a proposal for a major contract, also require extensive planning for successful outcomes.

- **A well-planned agenda is the first key to conducting effective meetings.**

  Starting a meeting without an agenda is like setting out on a journey over unfamiliar roads with no map and only a general idea of the route to your destination. You may get there, but only after lengthy detours. A good agenda defines the destination of the meeting, draws a map of the most direct route, and provides check-points along the way.

  An effective agenda also includes input from those who will be attending the meeting. This enables them to prepare ahead of time and provides better control over the content of the meeting. Their concurrence with the content makes it much easier to control the focus and flow of the discussion.

- **Ground Rules are the second key to conducting effective meetings.**

  Conducting a meeting without ground rules makes about as much sense as getting together a group of soccer, rugby, basketball and football players, and starting a "ball game" without telling anyone which game is being played. Each will assume he is playing his own, and chaos will result.

  Ground rules provide a means for agreeing on acceptable behavior and make it possible to control non-productive behavior. This can include long-winded dissertations, persistent negativity, or domination of the group by an individual. With ground rules, these behaviors can be confronted in an objective, impersonal, nonthreatening way. Ground rules also set standards for factors such as attendance, timely arrival, personal responsibility for preparation, and anything else that may be relevant to the group.

  Groups that meet regularly derive large benefits from establishing ground rules. But even one-time meetings will proceed more smoothly with a brief review of procedural guidelines at the beginning.

  Ground rules are especially effective when they become part of the corporate culture. However, it will not work to arbitrarily impose them by circulating a document. They must be developed and validated by those who use them, and then they must be enforced.

- **Meetings don't happen in a vacuum.**

  Meetings are an inherently political process. Events within a meeting are always influenced by the larger constraints under which individual participants must operate. Failure to recognize this reality, or ignorance of major political considerations, can doom to failure the outcome of a meeting.

  These political factors exist on a continuum, ranging from interpersonal to inter-corporate and societal. Staff meetings among subordinates of a single manager may be fraught with interpersonal rivalry for preferred status. Meetings involving representatives from different companies or divisions have obvious potential for conflicts of interest.

Many of the difficulties posed by these differences can be overcome by conferring privately between meetings. Focusing on achieving win/win outcomes, where all parties are able to meet their individual objectives, is also helpful. In most cases, a free flow of information between participants before the meeting is helpful. However, it would be naive not to realize that there are times, specifically in meetings involving negotiation, when providing too much advance notice or information can stiffen resistance and impair the process.

Many conflicts during meetings stem from the personal sub-agendas of participants, which often have little or nothing to do with the specific objectives of the larger group. Remember that these sub-agendas may be the primary motive for individuals to attend the meeting. Create synergy by acknowledging and supporting them as much as possible, when they are not in conflict with the overall agenda.

- **Lead by example.**
  Meeting leadership, like any other form, is subject to changing trends and personality differences among individuals. There are a few unchanging basics that bear repeating.

  1. Lead by example. Don't expect others to prepare better than you do, to arrive on time when you are consistently late, or to be concise when you ramble on. Be professional and be consistent.

  2. Don't fake a participatory, empowering style. Two of the most demoralizing things a leader can do are ignoring input after asking for it and micromanaging the fulfillment of assigned responsibilities.

  3. Use consensus appropriately. Don't waste time forming it when it doesn't matter, and don't be afraid to unilaterally make decisions that are your responsibility.

4. Know when to step back. The most effective leaders recognize the benefit of calling in an unbiased facilitator to assist with major decisions.

5. Leaders sometimes sit on the sidelines. Never underestimate the power of positive followership, and don't be afraid to jump in as a Back Seat Leader when the need arises.

● **Have fun!**
It is easy to get caught up in the pressure of the moment and take life far too seriously. This attitude increases stress, diminishes creativity and spontaneity, and generally lowers the quality of results achieved by the group. So lighten up! In general, the best results come from groups of people who are able to laugh together, see the humor in mistakes, and take joy in their labors.

As you read the suggestions and guidelines in this book, you will find many ways to apply them to make meetings you attend more successful. Keep the book handy and write down your growing list of ideas. Soon, with lots of laughs and considerable joy, you will find that you are meeting less and enjoying it more. Your results will be better than ever. In fact, you will have joined the ranks of the Meeting Masters.

Appendix

This appendix includes two case studies. They serve as examples of how the principles covered in this book actually work as they are used to change the way meetings are managed in organizations. These two specific examples were chosen because of the differences they illustrate.

In the first illustration, change begins in a very small and quiet way, with the actions of one courageous individual. His helpful example eventually inspires various task force members to begin using his technique in other meetings they attend, and change slowly begins spreading throughout the organization. This case is especially important as an example and a source of encouragement for those who would be back seat leaders, if they only knew just what to say and how to say it. The discussion explores reasons why the style used in this case study is especially effective.

In the second case, change is initiated at the top and deliberately implemented throughout the organization, with training and subsequent accountability fully supported by the C.E.O. This example is a road map of sorts for effecting change in corporate culture. Throughout the experience, input from everyone is solicited and attended to. Then, when everyone is satisfied that the system is workable, compliance is expected, and accountability is established.

Case Study One:
Back Seat Leadership Makes a Difference

Not long ago, a division president of EXCO Corporation decided that several benefits could be derived by having division employees become more involved in community projects. He formed a task force and solicited volunteers to serve on it.

Hal, a group manager, was selected to chair the task force. Mark, who was recently lured away from a major competitor to join EXCO, was one of the dozen professionals who volunteered to serve on the task force. The group was charged with the responsibility of finding ways to promote the company through community involvement. Other than that broad mandate, no further guidelines were given, and no timeline or method of accountability was specified.

The first meeting was chaotic, with no clear sense of purpose or direction. The discussion was dominated by Hal and three other members. After listening to them ramble on for an hour-and-a-half about their roles in community events and service organizations, several members, including Mark, started to leave. Hal quickly asked the group to decide on a future meeting date, which was set for two weeks later.

The second meeting was not much different from the first. There was no agenda, and no minutes were distributed, because none had been taken. Three members, including Mark, were absent from this meeting, and two were quite late in arriving. Finally, after nearly an hour of relatively aimless discussion, once again dominated by the few, several people began voicing discontent and frustration with the lack of direction and purpose. Someone suggested that the next meeting be dedicated to formulating a mission statement for the task force. Consensus on this idea was immediate. Once again, another meeting was scheduled to be held in two weeks.

After the first meeting, Mark wasn't sure he wanted to remain on the task force, but he decided to stick it out for another time or two, even though he would be out of town for the second meeting. He was relieved to see that a memo, serving as a sort of agenda, arrived before the third meeting. The memo stated that during the meeting they would draft a mission statement for the task force, identify strategies for implementing the mission, prioritize these strategies, and develop an immediate plan of action. This seemed like an ambitious set of objectives for a relatively short meeting, but at least it was a starting point. He wondered how Hal planned to handle the process of drafting the mission statement.

He soon found out. Hal apparently had no plans at all. The third meeting began as the second one had, with four missing members and three latecomers. The six people there began discussing ways of getting people to volunteer to do things. Finally, after twenty minutes, Mark realized that unless somebody exercised some back seat leadership, this committee would never define any objectives, much less achieve them. He thought for a minute and then intervened, beginning the following dialogue:

"Excuse me, Hal, but I was under the impression that we were going to work on a mission statement at this meeting. Are we still planning to do that?"

"Sure. I was just waiting for a few more people to show up."

"Well, I have a lot of other things I need to be working on, and I can't stay too much beyond an hour. I wonder if we could get started now?" he asked calmly.

"Sure. Who has some ideas? What sort of mission do we want to have?"

Mark immediately saw that the discussion would fall into disarray again within minutes. "Say, isn't there a flip chart pad in that case on the wall? How would it be if someone wrote down ideas as the rest of us brainstorm them? And maybe somebody could take some notes as we go along," he casually suggested.

This simple act went a long way toward focusing the discussion. Chris volunteered to take notes, and Sally offered to list the ideas. For the next fifteen minutes, Mark deftly guided the group as they discussed their purpose, vision, and what the group hoped to accomplish. Then he realized that half the group had become very quiet and didn't seem to be paying much attention.

"Say, excuse me for acting like a little bit of a facilitator here, but I notice that half the group isn't saying anything," he observed. "If this mission statement is going to work, it is really important that we all participate in the discussion. Jack, what are your thoughts on the ideas that are up here so far?"

Finally, after an hour of productive discussion, Mark summarized the progress they had made and asked for consensus on his accuracy. This was easily obtained with a couple of minor changes. Then he suggested that it might be time to quit for the day.

Hal then got agreement that the group would continue meeting at the same time and place every two weeks, and Mark intervened one more time. "Hal, I wonder if it might save you some time and make your job a little easier if we just quickly set the agenda for the next meeting right now, so people would know how to prepare?"

"Hey, that's fine with me. Whatever you want to do."

Kathy noticed that they hadn't finished drafting the mission statement, and there were still three other items on the current agenda they had paid no attention to. "Shall we finish this job and then move on to those others?"

"Well," said Mark, "that might be a little ambitious. How long do the rest of you think it will take to wrap up this mission statement?"

"Gosh, I think two or three more meetings!" said Jack. "Maybe if Chris could send around copies of the notes from this meeting right away, we could think about it a little bit between times and speed things up a little."

"No problem!" agreed Chris.

"Okay, so we are each going to gather our thoughts on additions and improvements to the work we have done so far, and then continue with the mission statement next time?" asked Mark.

With ready agreement, the meeting adjourned.

The next day Mark called Hal to discuss the meeting. "Hal, I hope I didn't step on any toes by jumping in the way I did yesterday. But in my last job I served on several committees like this, and I picked up a few tricks that really smoothed out the process."

"Hey, not at all. I really appreciated your help. I really haven't had much time to devote to this project, and if you have any other ideas about how to get the show on the road, I'd be more than happy to hear them!"

During the ensuing discussion, Mark agreed to facilitate further discussion, using his training and experience in developing team mission statements, goals, etc. He also suggested to Hal that the group spend a little time over the next two meetings formulating some ground rules for conducting and participating in these meetings. This was a novel idea to Hal, but one he welcomed.

Discussion

With Mark's assistance as facilitator during the next few meetings, the mission statement took shape. Task force members developed a clear vision of what they hoped to accomplish, along with implementation strategies and a plan of action for getting started. The group welcomed the idea of articulating ground rules, and their implementation did a lot to turn the budding grounds-well of frustration into enthusiastic participation.

Other positive changes occurred over the next several months, some flowing from Mark's facilitation style, and others as a direct result of the ground rules. For example, communication within the group became smoother, with fewer interruptions and more respectful listening. Conflict no longer seemed threatening, as win/win alternatives were sought. The agenda was taken more seriously, with the whole group sharing responsibility for developing and enforcing it. Task force members began looking forward to meetings, arriving on time and well-prepared.

Nearly a year after its inception, the group made a presentation to the executive staff to review accomplishments of employees who had been involved as volunteers in various projects. The president noted that it had produced results that far exceeded his hopes and expectations, and he expressed the hope that they would continue to expand their efforts indefinitely. The task force was featured in the employee newsletter, and the team members received awards during the annual division recognition dinner.

As pleased as he was with the tangible results of the task force, the president would have been even more pleased if he had known about the invisible results. As the task force matured and developed its smoothly running process, members began noticing the striking difference between task force meetings and most of the other meetings they attended. Without even realizing what they were doing, many began quietly following Mark's example of back seat leadership. Some of the positive changes they effected included establishing ground rules within other routine meeting groups, sharpening the use of agendas, and drawing out silent group members. They often took the lead in seeking win/win outcomes.

There are several reasons why Mark's example was so powerful. Notice that his tone was respectful and non-challenging as he initially questioned the purpose of the meeting. Rather than confronting Hal, he asked a question, "Are we still planning to do that?" This format gave Hal plenty of room to save face, and the opportunity to explain if he had changed his mind.

It is also important to note that as he asked the question, Mark's nonverbal signals were consistent with the wording of the question and reinforced the non-confrontational tone. If he had been visibly tense, or angrily glaring, Hal would have recognized a direct challenge, and probably reacted defensively.

Once he started, Mark didn't back off. When he perceived that he hadn't yet done enough, that Hal was not yet in firm control of the process, he intervened again with a suggestion for a better way to handle the process. He could have offered to make the lists himself. But in this case he preferred to remain more involved with the discussion than would have been possible if he were preoccupied with clarifying and recording input. Furthermore, his suggestion and subsequent request allowed two people to become more actively involved in the meeting.

At this point, it was natural for him to continue leading the discussion, a role he gracefully fell into. Hal was astute enough to allow things to take their course. If Hal had made any move to retain control of the discussion, Mark would have backed off and let him. Back seat leadership is never about power struggles and confrontation.

Mark was very low key in his facilitation role, seeming almost to deny his position. When he did make an overt intervention, he was a bit deferential about it, "... excuse me for acting like a little bit of a facilitator here..". This emphasized the temporary nature of his involvement. At the end of the meeting, when he prodded the group toward even greater productivity by suggesting that they formulate the next agenda, he once again framed the proposal as a favor to Hal, the busy official leader.

His final recorded act of back seat leadership was the follow-up phone call to Hal the next day. This was a winning move, regardless of Hal's state of mind. If he had been offended, this was a chance to clear the air. If he was indifferent, or better yet, agreeably receptive, it was a chance to proactively make further suggestions. Hal would then have the chance to adopt the ideas himself or delegate them to someone. As things stood, Mark had accurately perceived during the meeting the previous day that Hal would be open to suggestion. This conference was the first of many that set the task force on track to achieve their excellent results. As the project developed, Mark accepted many responsibilities and made a strong contribution to the group. The rest of the team understood that he was a powerful force, but his loyalty to Hal was obvious, and there was never any question that Hal remained "in charge."

A final note should be made about Mark's personality. He is not some paragon of sensitivity or assertiveness. He is just an ordinary person, rather quiet and a bit shy. He jumped in because he believed in the importance of what they were trying to do, and because he knew a better way to conduct meetings.

Case Study Two:
When Change Starts at the Top

Apex Corporation is a small, high-tech company, founded as an entrepreneurial enterprise several years ago by Don Emmet. Apex produces highly specialized computer components that are sold to manufacturers of computers and computerized equipment. The company has experienced rapid growth, with healthy earnings and a slowly expanding workforce.

Emmet currently serves as Chairman of the Board. Three years ago he brought in Ted Nolan as C.E.O., specifically to help reach his ultimate goal of taking the company public. Nolan convinced Emmet that the only way to keep the company's competitive edge sharp enough to attract the necessary investors was to focus on the quality of their product, so a consulting group was retained to guide Apex through the process of a Total Quality overhaul.

The evolution into the Total Quality paradigm had powerful results in many respects, but it generated virtual gridlock in the calendars of the executive staff as they dashed from one meeting to another. Quality Council meetings were held every other week. Management meetings to analyze and approve recommended process changes were constant and critical. Committee meetings to prepare appropriate policy change proposals were ongoing. A multitude of meetings were required to plan, review, and approve training needs and programs, and still others were necessary to consider the plethora of ideas employees submitted to the Suggestion System, to plan awards and recognition, and to take care of all sorts of other details.

These quality-related meetings were in addition to the usual trouble-shooting sessions, market strategy meetings, monthly and quarterly reviews, staff meetings, etc., that were still necessary. The management team averaged more than three meetings per day, and it became common for two or more managers to take turns standing in the back of the room, whispering into the telephone, or dashing between rooms, as they tried to participate in two meetings at once.

Things might not have been quite so bad if the meetings were smoothly run, with a predictable time schedule, but nothing could be further from reality. Mid-morning meetings always started late, because half the people weren't out of their early morning meeting until thirty minutes after the second one was scheduled to start. Since people seldom knew details of the agenda ahead of time, or who would actually show up, no one was prepared for the meetings. Discussions rambled, often dominated by the manager in charge, and frequently rife with conflict and confrontation. Crowded schedules caused many meetings to end before important decisions were made.

For awhile, it seemed miraculous that so many great results came out of these chaotic meetings. Unfortunately, the bag of miracles began emptying rapidly after a couple of years. More and more, people began skipping entire meetings, usually with no notice. They arrived later and/or left earlier than ever. Increasingly often, tempers flared, and stress levels zoomed.

When the issue of implementing Quality Improvement Teams arose, a process that would create the need for even more meetings, the system hit overload and totally jammed. Discussion became irrational and decisions impossible. Finally, the Quality Council decided that the meeting process at Apex was out-of-control, and steps must be taken to improve it.

As with any process, the first step toward improvement was to define the problem and identify the causes. The first step was easy enough. The proposed definition met with swift and unanimous approval: "Meetings throughout Apex are consuming too much time in proportion to the value of the results they produce." Identifying the causes was not so simple. Within half an hour, the Quality Council was bogged down again, and voice volume was escalating. Nolan adjourned the meeting in frustration and went back to his office, not sure what to do next.

As he sat pondering the problem, his eyes fell on a business card half hidden under the corner of his desk pad. It held the phone number of a consultant who had helped a colleague's firm make some dramatic improvements in the way they handled meetings. Nolan grabbed the phone and set up a meeting for a couple of days later.

The consultant listened carefully to Nolan's description of the situation, talked to other managers, and circulated a survey. When preliminary findings were presented, the Quality Council agreed that the following list of issues defined the major causes of the overall problem with meetings at Apex:

–   Meetings start late.

–   People arrive late and/or leave early.

–   Key people are often missing during all or part of meeting.

–   Agendas are not circulated ahead of time, and often not prepared at all.

–   Lacking an agenda, nobody prepares for the meeting ahead of time.

–   Meetings don't follow the agenda, when there is one. The discussion jumps around, and extraneous items are routinely introduced.

–   Interruptions are frequent and chronic.

–   Poor listening results in backtracking, repetition of points that have already been made, questions asked after answers are given, etc.

–   Side conversations are prevalent and distracting.

–   Phone calls are frequently taken in the meeting room, or subordinates interrupt, creating distractions.

–   Some participants are long-winded and repetitious in their discussion.

–   Managers frequently dominate.

- Decisions are often delayed for lack of necessary information.

- Many decisions founder for lack of agreement.

- People repeatedly drop the ball on follow-up.

In order to measure their progress toward improvement, ten managers were selected as a sample group to form a baseline of current performance. This was not a random sample. These individuals were chosen because they were the most diligent about keeping their personal planners up to date with records of how they spent their time, and this was the only available record of the amount of time spent in meetings. From these logs, together with any available minutes of the meetings available and personal notes shared by participants, the consultant was able to formulate a reasonable estimate of the average amount of time that had been spent in meetings by the management team.

To supplement this information and begin evaluating progress toward change, standard forms were devised to be used for drafting agendas and for recording minutes of all future meetings. These forms served several purposes. The agenda form made it easier to clarify objectives, expectations, participant roles, etc., for meetings. It was made available as a template in the word processing system on the network, so it could be used either in hard copy or electronically. The recorder form simplified the process of keeping minutes and provided a central record of attendance and time spent in meetings. It also furnished an accountability system for conformance to new specifications for meetings. Typical examples of these specifications include distributing a preliminary agenda, starting and ending on time, achieving objectives, etc. The completed form could also be photocopied and distributed to participants at the end of the meeting. This simplified the process of keeping everyone on track with follow-up, and updating those who were unable to attend.

The next step was to conduct half-day training sessions to introduce the new forms and basic meeting management strategies. This training began with the Quality Council. It was then attended by all managers and professional support staff. The idea of spending half a day in a training program initially met with considerable resistance from the over-scheduled managers. However, the preliminary data collected by the consultant easily convinced them that spending half a day in this training would save them hundreds of hours over the course of a year or two.

A secondary objective of the training was to gather input for a uniform set of meeting ground rules that would be adopted for use in all meetings at Apex. The consultant, who conducted the training, also facilitated the entire ground rule formulation process. After the initial input was gathered during the training sessions, a task force worked with the consultant to formulate a proposed set of ground rules. These were then circulated to all management and support staff for comment. After the task force reviewed the comments and made appropriate amendments, they were circulated again, providing another opportunity for anyone to comment. This process was repeated a couple of times until there was no further significant input.

At this point a "Meeting Reform Project Kickoff" was held for all managers and professional staff to officially activate the ground rules. After Nolan emphasized the importance of making meetings more cost-effective, each of them received a personal copy, and poster-sized copies were framed and hung in each conference room.

Over a period of weeks, the consultant spent several days attending various meetings in a coaching capacity to provide on-the-spot reinforcement of concepts covered in the training. When the discussion began to stray, individuals began to dominate, or obstacles began to surface, the consultant called "time-out" and had the group discuss the process. In most cases the ground rules were being violated. Participants quickly learned to internalize these rules, quickly pointing out infractions themselves.

To keep up the momentum that was building, nineteen people volunteered to attend a training course on Meeting Leadership and Facilitation. They represented a broad enough spectrum that most meetings at Apex then had at least one trainee in attendance to help keep them on track. In addition to the leadership training, other sessions were held on a voluntary basis on problem-solving and break-through thinking. These were quite popular, and eventually it is expected that everyone will attend them. Further courses on listening, presentation skills, and time management were being planned for the future. These topics also laid the groundwork for the Quality Improvement Teams that would soon be implemented.

Discussion
Old habits are hard to change, even behavior habits associated with meetings. Nobody could point to one day or week at Apex and say, "this was when things turned around." Over four months were needed to lay the foundation, conduct the training, and complete the ground rules formulation process. However, with the unflagging support of Ted Nolan and the Quality Council, the new concepts quickly took root. For example, people understood that the ground rules were there to stay and should be taken seriously. Nolan made it clear that he expected to be called on them as quickly as anyone else, and indeed he was. The fact that the general atmosphere at Apex was reasonably supportive to start with made it easier. People soon developed their own easygoing codes for nudging each other into compliance, and generally tried to make enforcement firm, but impersonal and nonthreatening.

The forms also took some getting used to. In the beginning there was considerable grumbling, especially by the more impulsive people who took pride in their supposed ability to wing things. This mandatory structure was introduced with a "try it for awhile and let's see how it goes" approach. Knowing that they would have the opportunity to reevaluate the system after three months made it easier to give it a fair try. Most of the initial grumblers were soon converted when they found how much time the seemingly restrictive process saved them. The three month evaluation was conducted by e-mail and resulted in a few minor adjustments to the content of the forms, but support for retaining them was almost universal.

As mentioned earlier, one of the purposes of the recorder forms was to provide a means of gathering data about the effectiveness of meetings. This data included the total number of meetings being held, the amount of time spent in meetings, and the percentage of meeting objectives that were achieved, i.e., "Make a decision about..." A statistically valid sampling process was defined to conduct this analysis, and an administrative assistant was assigned to collect copies of these forms and analyze progress in improvement on a monthly basis.

From the time the forms were put into use, improvement was steadily obvious. The most dramatic effects were the decline in the average length of meetings, and a rapid rise in the percentage of objectives achieved. However, the average number of participants per meeting also decreased slightly, and the total number of meetings being held declined somewhat over the period.

The reason for the rise in the percentage of objectives achieved was partially due to the fact that few formal objectives had been articulated prior to the beginning of the Meeting Reform Project. The new Agenda form provided the structure to ensure that this crucial planning step was not skipped, and the ability to set effective objectives increased with practice.

The attitude about meetings was dramatically different at Apex after nine months. Typical comments collected on a survey included: "We are meeting less and enjoying it more!"; "It is amazing how much better we listen to each other now."; "At first the forms seemed rigid and overwhelming, but now I see them as a form of liberation. They really save me a lot of time and have tripled the effectiveness of our meetings."; and "The ground rules are great. We hardly ever think about them anymore, because they have become so automatic. But what a difference they have made!".

The final step in the Meeting Reform Project was to identify certain types of meetings that would benefit from the use of a formal facilitator. The Quality Council tried using a facilitator for several meetings and decided the benefits far outweighed the cost. So a decision was made that an external facilitator would be used for all strategic planning sessions, meetings to make decisions about policy, and other meetings involving sensitive issues.

For Further Reading

Ailes, Roger, with John Kraushar. *You Are the Message: Secrets of the Master Communicators*. Homewood, Ill: Dow Jones-Irwin, 1988.

Banville, T. G. *How to Listen – How to Be Heard*. Chicago: Nelson-Hall, 1978.

Block, Peter. *The Empowered Manager*. San Francisco: Jossey-Bass, 1987.

Burley-Allen, Madelyn. *Listening: The Forgotten Skill*. New York: Wiley, 1982.

Buzan, Tony. *Use Both Sides of Your Brain*. Rev. Ed. New York: E. P. Dutton, 1983.

_____. *Make the Most of Your Mind*. New York: Linden Press, 1984.

Cohen, Herb. *You Can Negotiate Anything*. New York: Dell, 1980

Covey, Stephen R. *The 7 Habits of Highly Effective People: Powerful Lessons in Personal Change*. New York: Fireside, 1989.

_____. *Principle-Centered Leadership*. New York: Fireside, 1992.

de Bono, Edward. *Lateral Thinking*. New York: Harper, 1970.

Deep, Sam and Lyle Sussman. *Smart Moves*. New York: Addison-Wesley, 1990.

Doyle, M. and D. *How to Make Meetings Work*. New York: Wyden Books, 1976.

Fisher, Roger F. and William Ury. *Getting to Yes: Negotiating Agreement Without Giving In*. New York: Penguin Books, 1983.

Frank, Milo O. *How to Run a Successful Meeting in Half the Time*. New York: Pocket Books, 1989.

GOAL/QPC. *The Memory Jogger: A Pocket Guide of Tools For Continuous Improvement*. Methuen, Mass.: GOAL/QPC, 1988.

Gordon, Myron. *Making Meetings More Productive.* New York: Sterling Publishing Co., 1981.

Helgesen, Sally. *The Female Advantage: Women's Way of Leadership.* New York: Doubleday Currency, 1990.

Howard, V. A., and J. H. Barton. *Thinking Together: Making Meetings Work.* New York: William Morrow, 1992.

Kieffer, George David. *The Strategy of Meetings.* New York: Warner Books, 1988.

Kohn Alfie. *No Contest: The Case Against Competition.* New York: Houghton Mifflin, 1986.

Kushner, Malcolm. *The Light Touch: How to Use Humor for Business Success.* New York: Simon & Shuster, 1990.

LeBoeuf, Michael. Imagineering. New York: McGraw-Hill, 1980.

Peoples, David A. *Presentations Plus: David Peoples' Proven Techniques.* New York: John Wiley & Sons, 1988.

Reed, Warren H. *Positive Listening: Learning to Hear What People are Really Saying.* New York: Franklin Watts, 1985.

Senge, Peter M. *The Fifth Discipline: The Art and Practice of the Learning Organization.* New York: Doubleday Currency, 1990.

Smith, Terry C. *Making Successful Presentations: A Self-Teaching Guide.* New York: John Wiley & Sons, 1984.

Steil, Lyman K., Larry L. Barker, and Kittie Watson. *Effective Listening.* New York: Addison-Wesley, 1983.

Thomsett, Michael C. *The Little Black Book of Business Meetings.* AMACOM, 1989.

Thompson, Charles "Chic". *What a Great Idea! Key Steps Creative People Take.* New York: HarperPerennial, 1992.

The 3M Meeting Management Team. *How to Run Better Business Meetings: A Reference Guide for Managers.* New York: McGraw-Hill, 1987.

von Oech, Roger. *A Kick in the Seat of the Pants: Using Your Explorer, Artist, Judge and Warrior to Be More Creative.* New York: Harper & Row, 1986.

_____. *A Whack on the Side of the Head.* Menlo Park, Calif.: Creative Think, 1983.

Wycoff, Joyce. *Mindmapping: Your Personal Guide to Exploring Creativity and Problem-Solving.* Berkley Books, 1991.

Additional Resources

DAY-TIMERS®, Inc.
One Day-Timer Plaza
Allentown, PA 18195-1551
Phone: (215) 266-9313

Meeting Planners International
1950 Stemmons Freeway, Suite 5018
Dallas, TX 75207-3109
Phone: (214) 712-7700

Toastmasters International, Inc.
P.O. Box 9052
Mission Viejo, CA 92690
Phone: (714) 858-8255

Analytic Hierarchy Process:
Expert Software, Inc.
5001 Baum Blvd., Suite 600
Pittsburgh, PA 15213
Phone: (412) 682-3844, FAX: (412) 682-7008

Meeting Management Software:
QSoft Solutions Corp.
P.O. Box 556
East Rochester, NY 14445-0556
Phone: (800) 669-9701, FAX: (716) 264-9702

Applied Quality Methods
121 Freeport Road
Pittsburgh, PA 15238
Phone: (412) 826-1110, FAX: (412) 826-1120

Index

About the Author

Sharon Lippincott has twenty years experience providing workshops and consulting services. She has helped organizations of all sizes achieve continuous improvement in the way people communicate and work together. As a Director for the Council on Realizing Excellence in Management (CoREM), she specializes in interpersonal and group communication and problem-solving techniques.

After graduating with distinction from Boston University, she earned a master's degree in psychology from Central Washington University. She has taught courses at several colleges and universities, and is the author of dozens of published articles on professional development and self-improvement.

For Further Information

Thank you for your interest in this book. Your questions, comments, success stories and suggestions for revisions of this material are enthusiastically invited.

For information about program speeches by Sharon Lippincott and ways CoREM services can help your organization manage meetings more productively, please contact:

> CoREM
> 1776 McClure Rd.
> Monroeville, PA 15146
> e-mail: s_lippincott@hotmail.com

ORDER FORM

Meetings: Do's, Don'ts and Donuts
By Sharon M. Lippincott

Retail Price: $16.95 U.S.

Special Offer: 2 books for $30.50 U.S. *(Save 10%)*

Corporate Sales: **Please call for information on special corporate editions. Phone (412) 323-9320**

Shipping:
Book Rate: Add $2.50 for shipping for first book and $1.00 for each additional book. (Surface shipping may take three to four weeks.)

Priority Shipping: $5.00 for up to two books (Please call for priority shipping information on more than two books. Phone: 412-323-9320).

Terms: Payment with order.

Please send me _____ books. I understand that I may return any book for a full refund — for any reason, no questions asked.

Name: _____
Address:_____
City:_____State: _____ Zip: _____

Sales Tax: Please add 7% for books shipped to Pennsylvania address.

Amount Enclosed _____

Send Check or Money Order to:
Lighthouse Point Press
100 First Avenue, Suite 525
Pittsburgh, PA 15222